GET THE LOW-DOWN ON PAULA!

- What is Paula really like?
- Who is she dating?
- What kind of man does she find irresistible?
- How has Paula's rise to fame changed her?
- Is there an acting career in her future?

Packed with all the juicy details you want to know, this intimate biography tells all about Paula's friends and family, her favorite activities, her skyrocketing career, and her dreams for the future. You'll find it all here in this fun and fact-filled book!

PAULA ABDUL

GRACE CATALANO is also the author of the *New Kids on the Block Scrapbook*, which is available in a Signet edition. She lives on the North Shore of Long Island.

PAULA ABDUL
Forever Yours

Grace Catalano

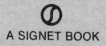
A SIGNET BOOK

SIGNET
Published by the Penguin Group
Penguin Books USA Inc., 375 Hudson Street,
New York, New York 10014, U.S.A.
Penguin Books Ltd, 27 Wrights Lane,
London W8 5TZ, England
Penguin Books Australia Ltd, Ringwood,
Victoria, Australia
Penguin Books Canada Ltd, 2801 John Street,
Markham, Ontario, Canada L3R 1B4
Penguin Books (N.Z.) Ltd, 182-190 Wairau Road,
Auckland 10, New Zealand

Penguin Books Ltd, Registered Offices:
Harmondsworth, Middlesex, England

First published by Signet, an imprint of New American
Library, a division of Penguin Books USA Inc.

First Printing, August, 1990
10 9 8 7 6 5 4 3 2 1

Copyright © Grace Catalano and Lamppost Press, 1990
Cover photo credit JJ/Star File

 REGISTERED TRADEMARK—MARCA REGISTRADA

PRINTED IN THE UNITED STATES OF AMERICA

To Michael and Mary
and the kids at the camp

Contents

Introduction

"She's all heart!"

—Lorraine, Paula's mother

In a relatively short period of time, Paula Abdul has achieved what others can only dream about. There is no limit to her talents. A successful dancer/choreographer since 1982, Paula proved she could do anything she set her mind to when she recorded her debut album, *Forever Your Girl*. She beat the odds and achieved her goals despite the discouragement she received along the way.

Though it took months for her album to hit *Billboard*'s Top 20 chart, once it made the list, it zoomed to the number one spot. *Forever Your Girl* would spawn seven hits and garner Paula with a carload of awards. Paula's debut album has become one of the most successful of the year, launching her as a major star on the music scene.

But Paula's music career is only part of her

life and accomplishments. Long before Virgin Records signed her to an album deal, Paula was working on an entirely different career. With a blink of the eye, she went from choreographer of other rock stars' videos to starring in her own. She is considered by many to be the best choreographer working today and is in such demand she is finding herself turning down more offers than she is accepting. Quite frankly, there aren't enough hours in Paula's day to do all the work being offered to her.

What is Paula Abdul's unbelievable appeal? Why does every rock star want her to choreograph their videos? More important, what does she have that sets her apart from the rest? For one thing, Paula is friendly and warm and has remained remarkably down-to-earth. Her deep brown eyes shine with self-reliance. Her contagious smile, vivacious personality, and disarming sincerity have established her forever in the hearts of music lovers. Though some critics were skeptical when her debut album was released, Paula isn't complaining. She is a living affirmation of the American legend: the success story.

She isn't an overnight star, but like all good show-business stories, Paula's has a fairy-tale ending. She refers to the recording of her first album as a turning point in her career. "Some people said, 'What is this choreographer doing singing?' " she recalls. "But I've always done things no one expected. If you told me to go right, I would go left. I'm very unpredictable.''

Her style and approach to stardom is a new phenomenon in the rock industry. Whereas some of her contemporaries display cool, hard-to-get-close-to images, Paula enjoys being in the spotlight. When the paparazzi see her at a restaurant or award show, she doesn't hide her face. When the cameras start to click, Paula isn't the type to dash past photographers. She stands still for a moment and flashes her trademark smile. The truth is, she really doesn't mind having her picture taken.

But there is more to being a public figure than simply posing for photos. Paula achieved her goals because of determination and drive. ''I've always had a fire in me,'' she says. ''I wanted to be onstage, singing, dancing, and acting from the time I was a little girl. And I knew I would get my chance someday.''

Paula started planning for success as a child growing up in the San Fernando Valley in California. A spunky, determined kid, she became interested in performing at age four after viewing Gene Kelly in the movie *Singin' in the Rain*. She decided right then and there that she wanted to become a performer, and nothing stood in her way from that day forward. She stepped onto a stage for the first time when she was seven and knew that's where she wanted to stay.

Paula is an overachiever who likes to branch out into all aspects of the business.

She isn't the type who is satisfied to stay at one level for too long.

"My mom always used to tell me, 'Have something you can fall back on,' " she says. "She told me that even though she supported my career and goal to be a performer, she still knew how unstable a show-business career could be."

When Paula was sixteen years old, she got a bit of encouragement from actor/dancer Gene Kelly, whom she met in a restaurant. "When I met Gene Kelly, I told him what an inspiration he was to my dancing career," recalls Paula. "He was so nice and encouraging. It meant a lot to me and gave me the drive to really give it a try."

Her big break was being chosen as cheerleader for the Los Angeles Lakers basketball team at just nineteen years old. A few months later, she was the group's leader and choreographer. Spotted by the Jacksons, Paula was recruited to choreograph their "Torture" video, and the sudden recognition put her in the mainstream.

Though she became a choreographer for other rock stars like George Michael, Duran Duran, and Janet Jackson, Paula was initially surprised that she was making a career at creating dance routines. "Choreography kind of fell into my lap," she confesses. "I didn't know it would be a career for me to make money—it was just something fun."

That "something fun" became Paula's ticket to the top. Her dances belong to her alone. You can always tell Paula's style. She is instinctively balletic in her dance steps, from her small gestures to her bounding leaps. There is a glow, definition, and ease to Paula's movements. A seemingly effortless performer, she is well-known for her tireless perfectionism. She spends infinite hours planning, rehearsing, and reshaping each of those routines that always seems so spontaneous. All this endless hard work gives Paula Abdul her breathtaking craftsmanship as a dancer. Her vehement determination never to repeat herself shows off her matchless versatility.

Paula can master every conceivable style of dance and often does. From modern to jazz to tap to street-wise funk, she creates routines that are distinctively hers.

Paula is reminiscent of the stars of years ago. The kind of stars who were talented actors, singers, *and* dancers. Today there are few who fall under that category. Dubbed "Gene Kelly of modern dance," Paula Abdul plans on breaking into film in the future—first in small supporting roles, then building to starring roles. Undoubtedly, a career in movies will secure her title of "all-around entertainer."

By any standards, Paula Abdul is now a superstar. The more popular she becomes, the more her name keeps popping up in magazines and newspapers. A sure sign of success, she has been mentioned in the ever popular Hollywood rumor mill. From romance rumors with everyone from Michael Jackson to Arsenio Hall to John Stamos to the stories that she has gotten plastic surgery on her breasts and lips, Paula has been advised that this means only one thing: she has arrived.

According to *Us* magazine's in and out list, Paula Abdul is *in* for the coming year. *Us* also picked Paula as one of the "Stars Who Turned Us On." She was on two *People* polls, as one of the 25 Most Intriguing People of the year and one of nine who will dazzle us with her style in the 1990s.

All this proves that you really can't compare Paula Abdul to anyone else. She has already made rock 'n' roll history with her debut album, and the future shows no signs of anything less than it's been.

So popular is Paula that her record company, Virgin, decided to release a rushed second album for her many fans. Titled *Shut Up and Dance*, it consists primarily of extended versions of her number one hits from her six-million-selling debut album. While Abdul works on her second all-new album, Virgin is hoping to keep her fans happy with this collection of remixed songs.

Paula Abdul's future seems guaranteed: a new album, a movie, a worldwide tour in the planning stages. Paula is only beginning to realize her full potential as an entertainer.

The question on everyone's mind is, What keeps Paula Abdul so focused, so enthused about every project she embarks on? Her answer is simple: "When you're performing, you occasionally get an idea of the number of lives you touch, of how many people support your work," she says. "And that acts as a very strong motivator."

A Natural Talent

"If there's anyone who reflects dance in the '90s, it's
Paula."

—Gilbert Cates, Academy Awards producer

Paula Julie Abdul was born to Harry and
Lorraine Abdul on June 19, 1963, a
sunny, summery day in Los Angeles. Her father was a livestock trader during Paula's
childhood. She says her dad's job led to her
decision to cut down on eating red meat, ex-
plaining she had already eaten enough of it
to last several lifetimes. Eventually, Harry
traded in his job and now owns a sand and
gravel business.

As a very young child, Paula's activities
were not completely out of the ordinary,
even though she did grow up in a musical
household. Her mother had worked as an
assistant to director Billy Wilder and was,
for a short time, a concert pianist before
giving it up to get married and raise a family. Music remained a very big part of Lorraine's life, and it was her decision to

expose her two daughters, Paula and her older sister, Wendy, to film and the arts.

Both girls enjoyed watching old movie musicals. Paula was mesmerized by it all—the dancing, the glamour, the singing, and the *fun*. "I remember when I was four years old sitting on the couch with my parents watching *Singin' in the Rain* on TV," says Paula. "I was just watching Gene Kelly have a great time and I can remember looking at my parents in the living room and saying, 'I want to do that.'"

Regarding it as a passing fad, Lorraine and Harry didn't consciously think about Paula's decision to enter show business. They didn't realize how serious their young daughter really was. But they soon found out.

Paula began watching all the old MGM musicals on TV. She loved all Gene Kelly's movies the best, especially *Singin' in the Rain, Anchors Aweigh,* and *An American in Paris,* but she had other favorite performers such as Fred Astaire and Judy Garland. Paula found herself becoming more and more curious about the art of performing. She realized she didn't just want to know about it—she wanted to do it herself. "I'd actually dream about being in scenes, singing and dancing with Gene Kelly," she says.

Abdul showed signs of natural talent from the start. Her mom recalls, "Even as a little one, she would sit and watch her sister's dance group. Then she'd come home and re-

16

create everything she saw. Show her once, and she had it."

In a way, Paula reminded Lorraine of herself at her age. Like her daughter, she had also been somewhat of a dreamer going after the things she believed in. Lorraine began taking piano lessons when she was four years old and was just as serious about mastering the keyboard as Paula was about learning to dance.

Paula feels she resembles her mother; she has her features, smile, and dimples. She claims she inherits her mom's bouncy personality, but Paula does have a lot of her dad's mannerisms, too. She has often thought of herself as a combination of her mother and father.

When Paula was seven, the bubble of the happy childhood she had known burst. Harry and Lorraine's marriage had slowly been falling apart, but they were trying to stay together for the sake of their two daughters. Lorraine was the first to see it coming, and the hurt she felt was multiplied by fear of what a divorce would do to Paula and Wendy. Looking back over the years of her marriage to Harry, Lorraine could only conclude that it was the old story of a guy and a girl falling in love before they were old enough to handle the responsibility of marriage. She knew she had loved Harry intensely when they were first married, and she believed he had loved her just as much.

They had two beautiful daughters together, and for a while Lorraine and Harry were blissfully happy. But something had changed, something was wrong, and there didn't seem to be any way out except to split up.

At the very young age of seven, reality suddenly crept into Paula's life. The impact of it was immense. She initially went through all the fears and changes that young children experience when their parents divorce. Paula loved both of her parents so much, and she couldn't understand why they had to change everything. She would now see one parent at a time. She knew nothing would ever be the same and she longed for her home life to go back to normal. She wanted her mom and dad to be happy again, but deep down inside, Paula knew that wasn't possible.

Paula and Wendy were raised by Lorraine in a comfortable middle-class condo in the San Fernando Valley community of North Hollywood. On weekends, Paula would see her dad and he'd try to make up for their lost time by taking his daughters out to an amusement park or the beach or a basketball game.

Thinking back on those years, Paula says, "It was very hard. I saw my dad only two days a week and I missed him a lot the other five days."

Paula's interest in performing increased after her parents divorced. Her desire to be on a stage would not go away, and Lorraine was faced with a decision. She really didn't want Paula in show business in any capacity. She particularly didn't think it was a good place for a child. She felt a child in show business would miss out on the normal activities of going to school, having friends over, and getting involved with sports. But she didn't have the heart to keep Paula away from trying something she obviously wanted to be part of.

By the time Paula was seven years old, she was performing with the local community theater groups. At eight, she began taking dancing lessons with Dean Barlow, who ran a dance studio in Hollywood. "That was a fluke," says Paula's mom on how she finally decided to study dance. "She was supposed to go to a friend's house. The mother called me and said she forgot her daughter had a dance lesson and wanted to know if she could take Paula. I said sure. I picked them up, and all I heard on the way home was, 'I have to take dancing.' "

Paula was anxious to learn everything about dance, and by the time she was ten, she was studying ballet, tap, jazz, and modern. Soon after, she won a scholarship to study under Joe Tramie and the Bella Lewitzky Company. "She could never miss a class," her mom says. "It could be pouring, the brakes on my car shot, and Paula was in the car with tears, afraid she was going to be late. Never mind that Mother is drowning and driving without brakes," concludes Lorraine, laughing.

It took only one performance onstage for Paula to know that performing was what she really wanted to do. Her favorite childhood memory is the time she entered a talent contest. She was so excited about showing off her singing and dancing to a live audience that she worked night and day on her routine. For Paula, the anticipation leading up to the night of the actual talent show was almost too much to bear. The day of the show seemed to last forever and she counted the time passing, minute by minute.

When it finally was time to go to the theater, Paula got all dressed in an adorable outfit. She arrived early and anxiously waited backstage until her name was called to perform. She sang and tap-danced to "Yankee Doodle Dandy" and won first prize. From that moment on, it was hard to keep Paula away from the stage.

At ten years old, Paula plugged all her creative energy into a host of after-school activities. Everyone from teachers to other students could see Paula's outstanding talents. Everyone got along with Paula. There was really no way you couldn't have. She was always so pleasant and friendly to everyone she met.

In the fifth grade, Paula managed to keep up her school grades and juggle several different extracurricular activities with ease. "I've always had the ability to do a lot of different things at the same time without compromising any of the quality," she says. Paula was a star member of her school choir, president of the square dance club, and a member of the speech and debate team.

But probably the most important project she got involved in was in junior high school, when she was chosen as the choreographer for the school production of the Broadway musical *Hello Dolly*. The drama teacher that year decided to put together a show completely utilizing the talents of the students. In the past, only kids who wanted to be actors and singers had been chosen to participate in school plays; this time, he was going to display the talents of the students studying musical instruments as well as other behind-the-scenes jobs.

The night the show was put on, no one in the audience realized they were viewing a piece of entertainment history. It was the first time Paula Abdul would choreograph a show.

In those early years Paula thought of choreography as fun. Being so athletic, she not only mastered every style of dance, but she also played softball and basketball all through school. She considered making up her own dance routines as a great way to exercise and be creative.

Paula had no idea she would become a successful choreographer. It was just one thing she loved doing, along with singing and dancing. She always had ideas for different dances and wrote them out on paper the way a child interested in art would sketch a portrait.

She would have never been able to choose

between performing and choreography because they were both great outlets for her to plug into. Fortunately, Paula Abdul never had to make that choice. In just eight years, she would be making a career out of dancing *and* choreography, and showing the world just how talented this little "Valley Girl" really was.

Miss Popularity

"Paula is always nice, always friendly."
—Marlon Jackson

Paula's preteen and teenage years prepared her for the life she is living today.
She spent most of her summers during those
years touring the country in summer-stock
productions. Though she often appeared in
relatively small roles in the plays, she loved
being in different theaters, milling around
backstage, asking questions, and soaking
everything in.

Lorraine traveled with Paula to some of
the theaters and kept a close eye on her
eager-to-learn daughter. Paula says her
mother and father were not the traditional
stage parents, but she did get support from
both of them.

When she thinks back on her junior and
high school years, Paula fondly describes
this whole period in her life as marvelous.
In junior high, Paula spent almost every af-

ternoon rehearsing in the school's auditorium for the numerous school plays she appeared in.

As she entered her sophomore year in Van Nuys High School, she wondered if she would experience any sudden changes, but everything remained the same. When tryouts for the new school drama production rolled around, Paula auditioned and won a role, just like she had done in junior high.

In tenth grade, Paula was involved in a whirlwind of activities. She tried out for the cheerleading team and was chosen, later becoming the squad's head cheerleader. "She used to have the girls come over in the backyard, and they would work, work, work," recalls Paula's mom. "Everything always had to look great."

Cheerleading and participating in school plays weren't the only things Paula gave her extra time to in high school. "I was the junior class president, homecoming princess, and May queen," she offers, "all that disgusting high school stuff, but I loved it."

Paula also loved making new friends and dating. Today she still keeps in contact with some of her closest high school friends. "My friends from school don't look at me or perceive me any differently now from how they did when we were in school together," says Paula. "When I see them, we never discuss my career. We just talk about normal, day-to-day things. Some of my friends were voted Most Likely to Succeed in high school, and now they're the ones who settled down, got married, and are perfectly content being moms and dads. My high school boyfriend is now married and has a baby," she adds, finding it hard to believe.

Paula was a highly academic girl in school. She let her emotions out on stage or cheerleading, but Paula was really quite shy. Her early years were inspired by the feelings she had from watching old musicals and listening to Broadway show records. She enjoyed reading books and learning. "It was my mom who taught me it's good to have something to fall back on, and that's why school became so important to me," she says. "I never got tired of learning new things."

By the time Paula was a senior in high school, she was completely wrapped up in wanting to become a performer. For a while it was all she thought about. She had a lot of energy even back then and a bundle of talent that she couldn't wait to unleash on the world.

Everyone was aware of Paula all through high school. She was pretty, her personality was a combination of shyness and perkiness, and she seemed so mature and sure of the things she wanted. She was more serious than other students; she was always dreaming and planning and thinking ahead.

In 1981, Paula graduated from Van Nuys High School with a 3.85 GPA and a scholarship to Cal State at Northridge. She wanted to go to Broadway and go after her goal of becoming a star, but was getting discouragement everywhere she turned.

No one thought Paula could make a career out of dancing. She was only 5′2″ tall and many skeptics told her she was too petite for the dance world. "Even though she'd out-dance everyone," explains Lorraine, "Paula never fit anyone's idea of a tall, leggy dancer. She went through lots of rejection, but she had the drive and determination."

For the time being, Paula decided to take her mother's advice and begin college in the fall. Her major was in TV and radio. "I was studying to become a sports broadcaster," she says. "I thought I'd become the next Jayne Kennedy."

And so Paula Abdul's real goal was put temporarily on hold. Though her mom was happy that she was in college studying for a career in broadcasting, Paula felt something was missing. After years of taking dance lessons, she was finding it difficult to just turn everything off because some people were telling her it was nearly impossible. Paula had faith in herself and that's what really counted.

Somehow Paula's vision to enter show business was never dimmed by the thought that it might be difficult to get ahead. When it came to succeeding at her goals, she was fearless. "In the back of my mind, I always knew I'd make it somehow," she explains.

Knowing she would get her chance, she decided to stray temporarily away from her dancing dreams. Though she kept up with her dancing privately, she hadn't been on a stage for five months. She was a freshman in college and decided to indulge herself in studying.

But all that would soon change. One of Paula's friends persuaded her to try out for the Los Angeles Laker cheerleading squad. Paula's professional career was about to begin, but it wouldn't be on a concert stage as she had imagined. Instead, it would be on the polished floor of the basketball arena at Los Angeles Forum.

Laker Girl

"When she auditioned to be a Laker Girl, Paula was such a great dancer, really slick. Within three weeks she became the choreographer. I think we even gave her a raise from $500 to $550 a month."
—Lon Rosen, Laker publicist who hired Paula

Paula Abdul almost didn't try out for the Laker cheerleading squad. The day she arrived at the auditions, five hundred girls were there, all hoping to do the same thing.

"When I saw all those girls, I said no," recalls Paula. "I started to leave." As she was walking out of the building, something called her back. She didn't know it then, but she almost walked out on the one break that would lead to her current success.

"I turned around, went back in, and thought, 'I'll go in and watch at least,'" she says. After a few minutes of watching, Paula decided to try out. She did it, she says, for "self-satisfaction." Now she smiles at the memory. "It's a great thing that I did because I was chosen."

Out of the five hundred girls auditioning that day, only twelve would become Laker Girls—and Paula Abdul would be one of them!

Though she seemed shy and didn't know much about what they were looking for, she had a refreshing quality. She hadn't realized her full potential yet, but Lon Rosen knew that she wasn't like anyone else auditioning that day.

Rosen, who was then the publicist for the Lakers and now Magic Johnson's manager, hired Paula, referring to her one-minute audition as dynamite. "She was such a great dancer," he says, "really slick. Within three weeks she became the choreographer. I think we even gave her a raise from $500 to $550 a month."

Paula was surprised that becoming a Laker Girl would be a career for her. After taking over as choreographer of the team, she was given freedom to express herself and regarded this experience as a great training ground.

"It was the perfect outlet to experiment with different ideas that I had," she says. "I was this cheerleader who kind of broke the rules. I wanted to get rid of the pom-pom thing and focus more on dance. This stereotypical cheerleader thing always bothered me a lot—T&A, teased-up hair, and sexy bodies. It didn't matter how well you danced. Nothing mattered as long as you were a beautiful bombshell. I *never* was that, and I was always the underdog. I used to get yelled at by some of the people in the upper echelon of the Lakers organization. They'd say, 'Come on, Paula, you're picking a great dancer, but is she going to look great in her uniform?' "

Talent always meant more to Paula than good looks. And she didn't mind speaking her mind about it. She designed dazzling, innovative routines for the Laker Girls, taking the squad out of the realm of traditional cheerleading gymnastics. She had an originality no one had ever seen before, and her expertise as a dancer changed the way all future Laker Girls did their routines during the basketball games.

Paula's accomplishment was to take this group of cheerleaders and transform them into a dance team. As she explains, "I wanted to make them the best they could be."

Nineteen eighty-two was a busy year for Paula. With all the newfound excitement of being a Laker Girl, she was unsure if she should treat it like a part-time job and stay in college or give it all her time.

She opted to drop out of school so she could devote her entire day to dancing and choreography. Her mother wasn't happy with her decision, but Paula assured her she could always go back to school if she had to. Paula had been given an incredible opportunity to prove her talents, and she wasn't going to let it slip by. She was going to work around the clock if that's what it took to catch some attention.

Paula's philosophy on success is "You can *really* achieve whatever you want in life with a little hard work. To be in the entertainment business, you really have to be devoted to whatever area interests you. For me, I wanted to be an all-around entertainer from the time I was very young and I worked one hundred percent toward it."

Paula Abdul was a "budding celebrity"; she had achieved her first goal in the entertainment world. She had broken free from what others said. She had found success as a dancer despite the fact that she was just 5'2" tall. Paula's life would never be the same again. As a young girl dreaming of success, Paula often wondered, What if I hadn't gotten that lucky break or wasn't there at the right place at the right time? Now she wouldn't have to wonder ever again.

As a Laker Girl, Paula Abdul was leading the only life she desired. She was working at something she completely enjoyed and meeting celebrities who held season tickets to the Laker games.

It was at this time that she met Arsenio Hall, the popular late-night talk show host and a self-described "basketball freak." Paula and Arsenio shared many things in common and became good friends. In Arsenio, Paula found someone she could talk to about everything. He was equally ambitious, waiting for the day when his name would become a household word.

But his climb to the top was slow. Born the

son of a Baptist preacher and raised by his mother, grandmother, and godmother in Cleveland, Arsenio dreamed of achieving stardom as a comedian from the time he was twelve years old. He graduated from Kent State University with a bachelor's degree in speech. He worked as a salesman for a Detroit company that makes Noxema before getting some lucky breaks from singers Nancy Wilson and Patti LaBelle.

He lent his comic talents to a host of television projects, beginning in the summer of 1983 when he co-hosted the ABC-TV series *The ½-Hour Comedy Hour*. He was Alan Thicke's co-host on *Thicke of the Night* in 1985, was writer on Smokey Robinson's *Motown Revue* in 1985, co-hosted *Solid Gold* with Marilyn McCoo in 1986, replaced Joan Rivers on *The Late Show* in 1987, and finally launched his own show, *The Arsenio Hall Show*, on January 3, 1989.

"Arsenio is one of my dearest friends," says Paula. "I hang out with him whenever there's time to hang out. We enjoy each other's company. I can talk to him about anything. He means a lot of different things to me in my life. He's the one person I can tell exactly how I'm feeling; and he can understand it because he's either going through it or he's gone through it."

Arsenio always has something complimentary to say about his pal Paula. He remembers the first day he saw her. "Had Paula mentioned the words 'double platinum' back when she was a cheerleader, people would have called her crazy," he says. "But the little cheerleader beat the odds."

Paula has always been able to charm people. She is vivacious and her high spirit is infectious. She loves to laugh and has a great sense of humor. People respect her drive to be "on top." As a Laker girl back in the early 1980s, Paula was working hard and people were beginning to notice her.

Looking back on the dance routines she designed for the team, she says, "I'll watch old footage and I'll see something and say, 'That's pretty cool. I can update that a bit and make it even better.' "

There is one funny routine that stands out in Paula's mind. "We were all dressed in funny fat-men outfits," she remembers. "But when we ran onto the court, one girl bumped into Magic, and a bunch of us fell over like dominoes. I laughed so hard, and, well, I have the weakest bladder. It was *so* embarrassing."

Those moments were few and far between. Most of the steps the Laker Girls did were outstanding. After two seasons of strutting her stuff in the Los Angeles Forum, Paula received what would be her next "big break."

The Jacksons were looking for a choreographer for the "Torture" single off their *Victory* album. They liked the style of the Laker Girls' routines and decided, after a game, to find out who the choreographer was.

Paula was introduced to the Jackson brothers and taken aback by the compliments they showered her with. Jackie told her how impressed he was with the work she did with the Laker team. Then he asked her if she would be interested in working with the Jacksons on their video.

Was she interested? Paula could hardly believe her ears. She had been spotted by the Jacksons, a group she greatly admired, a group considered by many to be the biggest talent in the music world. They wanted her to choreograph their steps? She stood and looked at the brothers for a few seconds, grinning from ear to ear and said yes, she was interested.

The stage had been set. Paula was now on the brink of having even more people know her and her dance routines. There was no turning back now. Paula Abdul had already met the men who were to play crucial roles in her dynamic rise to stardom.

You've Got Me Dancing

"Madonna can shake it up, but she ain't no Paula Abdul. *She* shakes it up the way we shake it up in the ghetto. And that's saying something."

—Arsenio Hall

"The first day I was to work with the Jacksons, I was very nervous," admits Paula. "I let them know I wasn't an experienced choreographer, and they were very supportive."

Dancing had always come naturally to Paula. She never had to struggle with her routines. Her dances were full of vigor and flair, and sometimes she experimented with intricate choreography. Jackie Jackson admired the fact that Paula never took an easy way out. Her choreography was athletic and difficult. It required hours of rehearsing to make Paula's steps look easy on camera.

Her first day working with the Jacksons were filled with nerves and excitement. All

37

the brothers—Jackie, Jermaine, Tito, Marlon, Randy, and Michael—immediately tried to put Paula at ease. "I was just completely blown away," she says about the experience. "Michael Jackson is one of my favorite performers. He's got the all-around energy!" The Jacksons and Paula was a felicitous pairing. They complemented each other so perfectly and worked together in such harmonious teamship.

Paula had made a good first impression on Jackie and Marlon, who personally selected this relative unknown and put her in the limelight. The position of choreographing a music video for the Jacksons promised Paula invaluable exposure, since this group was a popular staple in rock music.

Paula didn't let the Jacksons down. She was every bit as professional and talented as they had anticipated. She not only worked well with the group, but she also became friends with them. In fact, her friendship with Jackie, in particular, became something for the gossip rags to pick up on.

Because Jackie was going through a divorce at the time, the rumors spread that Jackie and Paula were secretly dating. Once a piece of gossip like that leaks out to the public, it is completely embellished on until the parties involved publicly put an end to it.

In this case, it was the first time Paula had been mentioned in the gossip columns. At first she was upset about the rumor that she and Jackie were lovers. It bothered her for a while, but then she shrugged it off. She wasn't used to people talking about her life like that, but she figured the people who knew her would know the truth. Today, Paula laughs at such rumors by saying, "There was nothing going on between Jackie Jackson and me. We were just good friends."

What Paula shared with Jackie and the rest of the Jackson brothers was an abiding love of music and a drive for fame and success. There was a great love between Jackie and Paula, but not the kind the rumors suggested. They had a unique respect and love and involvement with each other.

Paula could always get along best with people who shared her interests. When she was in the presence of another entertainer, she could talk endlessly about dancing and style and music.

Working with the Jacksons was a dream come true for Paula. She freely admits she learned as much from them as they did from her. Each benefited from the other's talents—Paula from the Jacksons' fame, reputation, and knowledge of the music business, and the Jacksons from Paula's innovative dance routines.

In 1984, the Jacksons embarked on a world tour. Their *Victory* concert was one of the biggest shows of the year, and Paula's snazzy dance steps played a big part in it. When her work with the Jacksons was completed, she returned to the Forum and got back on line with the Laker Girls. It was where she thought she would stay, but fate was about to play another hand in her career.

The "Torture" video had brought Paula attention. It was no secret that the Laker cheerleader in the center of the line was the choreographer of the Jacksons' new video. She felt very fortunate to have been part of the Lakers' cheerleading team and to have met the Jacksons. "It was the work with the Lakers that first opened all the doors for me," she says. "I'll always be grateful to them and the Jacksons for giving me those first important breaks."

Paula was given the chance to be creative and inventive; she was able to reach inside and provide vibrant, alive dance steps which would, in turn, make her one of the most sought-after choreographers in the business.

John McClain was a black music executive promoted to vice-president of A&M Records. He was about to shape a new career for another member of the Jackson family by creating an all-new image for the baby of the close-knit clan—Janet Jackson. Janet was putting the finishing touches on her third album, titled *Control,* and McClain was in the process of inventing an entirely different look for her. He was responsible for selecting her loose, gangster-black suits and weighty gold prizefighter belts.

Paula's style was exactly what McClain was looking for. He had been to a few Lakers games and studied the steps of the cheerleaders. The style was new, fresh, and something he felt would be a major success in the music world.

For the videos of Janet's songs, McClain had envisioned mini musical productions, and he needed someone who could furnish arresting dances that would separate Janet from her competition. After watching a score of dancers perform, McClain decided only one individual would be able to dream up new, innovative steps for Janet. And that one individual was Paula Abdul.

The Right Moves

"I'm very happy about Paula's success. She's like a sister to me, and there's no competition between us."
— Janet Jackson

Paula Abdul remembers the day she met John McClain. "He was a season ticket holder of the Laker games, and I met him toward the end of the season," she says. "After one of the games, he approached me and said, 'I love what you do with the Laker Girls. I want you to put that style on an artist we have—her name is Janet Jackson.'"

The result of this dynamite teaming would bring Paula Abdul an overwhelming amount of recognition and firmly secure her name in show business. Paula's work with Janet Jackson would not only be her major breakthrough but also Janet's. As unbelievable as it may seem, Janet Jackson's name before her success with *Control* was synonymous only with the phrase "Michael's younger sister." Even though Janet had been in the business since the tender age of seven, she hadn't proved she could do it alone without the help of her family.

Janet, being the youngest member of the Jackson family, practically grew up on a concert stage, making unannounced appearances during the Jackson Five's shows. Although Janet's first ambition was to become a jockey, her father asked her at age seven to sing with the rest of her talented family. Joe Jackson wanted his youngest daughter in the family business and did all he could to be sure she started making records before she was out of her teens.

When Janet was sixteen, her father maneuvered a recording contract with A&M Records, despite the reports of his daughter's reticence. She didn't want a career in music; instead she wanted to try her hand at acting. She appeared on the TV series *Good Times, A New Kind of Family, Diff'rent Strokes,* and *Fame.* Her one season on *Fame* would be the last time she would work as an actress.

Deciding to pursue a serious music career, Janet's first two albums, *Janet Jackson* (1982) and *Dream Street* (1984), were not the successes she wanted. It was her third album, *Control,* that brought Janet the recognition she deserved.

At the time of its release, Janet considered it to be "a declaration of independence. I wanted to do this on my own. I wanted to prove something to myself," she said in an interview on *Good Morning America.* "I just wanted to see it happen because of me. I wanted to know that the public wasn't interested because my brother wrote this song but because of me. I wanted my own identity."

In her four videos off the *Control* album, it was Paula Abdul who would help give Janet Jackson the identity she longed for. Paula understood Janet's feelings and she was able to transform them into the now famous rubbery dance moves she created for the singer.

In a 1986 interview, Paula said, "I was kind of scared to see what would happen when I started giving her some steps. But immediately Janet would say, 'Come on, Paula, you dance first,' and I thought, Wow. So I'd just start dancing and she'd say, 'I like that, Paula.' I'd break up the steps to show her and she'd pick it up.

"Janet's music had such a great beat," continued Paula. "The way she was dancing, I knew my style of choreography would work really well with her. I use a lot of isolations, and my choreography and Janet's music fit together so perfectly."

Paula decided to mix concepts almost unheard of in the world of dance. McClain didn't ask Paula to choreograph just one video; he wanted her to create an image for Janet. Paula was signed to work on dance routines for four of Janet's videos, and she wanted to do something completely out of the ordinary.

In order to build an individual style for Janet, Paula soaked up every kind of move she saw, from the street to the dance clubs. "Artists are taking a lot from what comes off the street and that's where most of my inspiration came from," she said at the time.

"When I first started working with Janet, a whole new style was brought out," she explains. "It was a combination of what I was doing with the Laker Girls. My idea with the Lakers was to combine elements of jazz and technical training with street funk. When I was approached to work with Janet, her music inspired me to go a little further with the style. Everyone thought I was crazy, but once Janet's videos were seen, that's when everything hit."

The Janet Jackson videos she choreographed ("When I Think of You," "Control," "Nasty," and "What Have You Done for Me Lately") put Paula Abdul on the map. She was setting a new style for dancers, and her efforts won her both critical and public acclaim. Paula filled every second of Janet's songs with the most gymnastic and expansive choreography ever presented on any video, and it wasn't going unnoticed.

Even though she went on to work with other talented singers, Paula considered Janet to be the most determined of the bunch. "Janet's my prize student," Paula says. "She worked her butt off for me. The end result is that we made each other look extremely good.

"With Janet's videos I really got to see the influence choreography has on kids and adults," she continues. "Going to clubs and seeing people emulate the steps—as if they put the videos on slow motion, pause, freeze. 'I'm gonna get that step!' They were doing the *exact* choreography. It blew me away.''

Paula remembers how she created the dance that would later be called the Snake in dance clubs across America. ''I happened to be in Atlanta when I was working with Janet,'' recalls Paula, ''and I saw this kid doing this weird body movement with his neck and shoulders. I couldn't tell what he was doing, but I could isolate the movements in my own body. So I taught it to Janet, we put it on a video, and suddenly people were doing it and calling it the Snake.''

As soon as Janet's videos began playing, everyone became aware of Paula Abdul. Word spread quickly about this hot new talent. It seemed everyone wanted to snatch her up for one project or another. Paula's days with the Laker Girls were over, and her career as a full-fledged choreographer was about to begin.

Paula regarded the work pouring in as a ''snowball effect. It was nonstop for me,'' she says. When she wasn't in the studio choreographing videos, she was giving pointers on movement and style and preparing rock stars for upcoming concert tours. Paula's students are some of the hottest names in the business: Duran Duran, Steve Winwood, George Michael, INXS, Aretha Franklin, the Pointer Sisters, Luther

Vandross, Kool and the Gang, and Dolly Parton.

She created the Velcro Fly dance for ZZ Top's song of the same name. "That was right after my work with Janet," says Paula. "And it was going from one extreme to the other, in a completely different direction."

Paula was hired on a day's notice to choreograph the dance in Debbie Gibson's "Shake Your Love" video. "I had one day to put it all together, then boom, video time," recalls Paula.

She helped actors Dan Aykroyd and Tom Hanks on the video for their movie *Dragnet*, and now Hanks tells Paula, "My biggest claim to fame is that you once choreographed me."

As for the *Dragnet* dance, Hanks explains, "Luckily, it was only two very easy blocks. Paula would say, 'Here's the first block, here's the second. Okay, now here we go.' But even that you can screw up enough times to have to do it a million times over and over again."

With every artist she worked with, Paula had a routine she would go through before even beginning to create dance steps for them. "I would have creative meetings with the artist and the record to find out what directions they wanted to go in," she says. "Then I studied all the footage from previous tours and videos to see what their natural movements were. From there I built on that natural framework to try to create a style that would be all their own."

While others see Abdul's choreography as genius and ground breaking, she sees it as "extremely athletic, combining a careful balance of femininity but also 'I can do what the guys can do.' When I choreographed that style for Janet, it worked really well for her and it went with the music. My choreography suits men very well, and the women who can do it are damn hard, strong dancers."

Paula Abdul was now in demand—and the amount of work being offered to her was not letting up. It seemed everyone wanted her to work on *their* project. Paula took on an impossible workload, but she managed to handle it. She fit every job into her schedule, even if it meant getting very little sleep. Paula was emerging as the fastest-rising choreographer in the world of music, and she wasn't going to let one job slip by. Every project Paula accepted was just one more step on her ladder of success.

Of her new career as a video choreographer, Paula says, "It was mind-boggling to me to get paid really good money for something so fulfilling."

The appeal of Paula Abdul's work was rapidly growing, so much so that she was being approached by big movie studios, directors, and producers who wanted her to bring her dances to the silver screen. Because she was new to the business, Paula had no representation at this time, no agent or manager to handle the offers and the legal affairs. She did it all on her own.

The way some people found her was through the telephone book, where her mom's name and number were listed. Paula would be working all day and receive a call from her mom telling her she was getting phone calls from major studios. "My mom would say, 'Paula, Paramount Pictures is on the line. They're asking me what your rates are. What do you want me to tell them?'" begins Paula, laughing at the memory. "And I would say, 'Just pretend you're my agent, I don't know, just make up something.'"

Everything was moving so fast for Paula, she really wasn't aware of how well-known she was becoming. She found out after hanging up on Aretha Franklin—and hearing about it later. Aretha thought she'd give Paula a buzz to ask her if she'd help in choreographing her upcoming tour. When Paula answered the phone, she figured it *had* to be a practical joke. "A voice said, 'Is Paula Abdul there? This is Aretha Franklin.' I said, 'Yeah, sure,' and hung up," recalls Paula. "I didn't believe it was her. She called *herself?*"

There is something special about the beginning years of every successful career. There is something innocent about it, when someone who will go on to become a huge success is just getting started, testing the waters, learning about how to handle themselves. For Paula, those early years of recognition were an exciting time. Like a babe in the woods, Paula was on the threshold of major success and she was enjoying every minute of her rise to the top.

When she speaks about those years, she gets a wistful look in her eyes. "It was a crazy time, but it was wonderful."

While Paula was still being hired to choreograph music videos, she was beginning to lend her talents to movies, and then to television for *The Tracey Ullman Show*. Her schedule was hectic, but Paula didn't mind. "When it started proving to be successful for me, I really stayed focused in that area," she comments.

She was building up her credits—and her contacts. She was hired to choreograph scenes in movies beginning with the futuristic thriller *Running Man* with Arnold Schwarzenegger; over the next three years, she would choreograph the bar scene in *Bull Durham* and act as dance choreographer for *The Karate Kid Part III* and *She's Out of Control*.

But Paula's favorite film assignment was working with Eddie Murphy and her friend Arsenio Hall in *Coming to America*. Murphy personally phoned Paula to tell her he wanted her to choreograph the African dance scene in the beginning of his movie. "It was terrific being on the set with Eddie and Arsenio," says Paula, "even if Eddie was too scared to learn to dance from me."

Like others in the business who met Paula, Murphy had complete respect for her. She was now the talk of the town, the new sensation, just as he had been years earlier.

Like Arsenio, Murphy has also become a close friend to Paula. He describes her as "a real sweet girl."

In a short time she had gained the respect and admiration of nearly every entertainer she met. She should have been very content with her achievements—and she was. But Paula still wasn't completely satisfied with her status. Even though she enjoyed working with other artists, she wanted more. She couldn't avoid the fact that she was hoping to get on a stage and choreograph her own dance steps. "Deep down inside, in the back of my mind, I knew this was an avenue for me to do other things. I always had the desire and dream to be onstage," she says with the utmost honesty.

Of course, Paula's dream was realized when she was a young girl, performing at dance recitals, in talent contests, and in school plays. And somehow as much as she thought that her desire might disappear, it didn't. It was still there. She was still yearning to sing and dance.

"I've always wanted to record an album of my own," she says, "and the more I worked with other artists, the more I wanted to do it."

Working with Janet Jackson made Paula realize that a music career of her own was possible and could be a lot of fun. While she was working with Janet, Paula would sing her songs and Janet would tell her, 'You should seriously consider singing.' "

Paula didn't need much more persuading

than that. She had already thought about it for a long time and made up her mind. She wouldn't discuss her dreams with anyone, but recording her own album was something she wanted to do eventually. In 1986, one reporter asked Paula if she wanted to become a singer in the future. Her answer was: "I think right now I want to get my career more in order and be the best choreographer, and from there, we'll see what happens."

Two years later, her instincts told her to try breaking into music. She had a lot of different ideas, but right now they were scattered. There was no time for rest and relaxation; Paula was at the crossroads of her career and she wanted to take the road that would help her branch out.

She was about to make her dreams become a reality, but didn't know what approach to take. She had already created the most innovative dance steps for other performers. Not wanting to think too much about the dance steps she would create for herself, Paula first began looking for songwriters, producers, and a few back-up singers. She decided to take it step by step; she knew everything would eventually evolve with time.

Paula wanted to record a demo, but wanted the song to make a strong impact on record executives. It would be all they would have to judge her talents on. Most young singers or bands trying to make a name for themselves spend countless nights traveling from one city to the next, playing small clubs. In the music business that's the way most record contracts are drawn up. Record executives like watching a performer on a stage in front of an audience. To some extent, even the most talented singers must have a certain connection with the audience in order to become stars.

A concert by a new artist shows their stage style, the way they perform in small or large clubs, whether or not they have overall technique as a performer. Most executives feel this end of the music business is important to the performer's longevity. The singer has to possess some kind of electricity to get noticed.

Paula Abdul had never given a concert, but she had been on stages and she had performed at the Lakers games. She was singled out by the Jacksons and John McClain at these games, but now she was going into a completely different ball game. She didn't want to sit on the sidelines anymore; she wanted to be out there center stage proving to the world what she could do as a performer.

Would she make as strong an impact as a performer as she had as a choreographer? Would the ball come down in Paula's court? She was about to find out!

Shooting For the Stars

"Paula is as great as everyone says. Her ambition
hasn't let her down yet. There's no reason to suspect
she'll fail now."

—James Brooks, Executive Producer,
The Tracey Ullman Show

In the world of popular music, it may often
appear as if fame and wealth are available
to the newest hot prospect who passes by.
Every few months a new contender for stardom bursts onto the scene from nowhere to
become the next superstar. Enormous record sales follow, a mass of critics, writers,
and photographers take notice, and in most
cases all the success and hoopla over the
new superstar is over in a few more months.

No one has ever pinpointed the reason
why someone with so much promise would
rise one minute and fall the next. Perhaps
the lack of *real* talent, experience, and a
good foundation in music could be some
reasons. Whatever the cause, throughout
the history of music there have been too

many shooting stars zooming to the world of fame and fortune, then falling into oblivion.

That is one kind of success in the recording industry, but there is also another. There are the performers who don't rush into a career without previous knowledge of the business. There are those who take a gradual but steady course to the top. There are the performers who first gain their experience and then branch out into other areas until they are satisfied with the end results.

There are the performers who, like Paula Abdul, don't follow fads or trends or rules, but stick by their own beliefs. Paula had seen all aspects of show business by the time she decided to break into the music business. She had honed her craft by working with other performers and was now ready to conquer the one field she hadn't yet tried.

Once the idea was set in motion, Paula started thinking about her new career. Creating her own music enveloped her every thought. The only problem, in the beginning, was what kind of music she wanted to sing. It had to be high energy, she decided, so she would be able to choreograph steps for herself. And it had to have a certain amount of commercial appeal, a cross between rock and rap. In a sense, Paula wanted her music to reveal her own personality.

Because she didn't write songs, she contacted people she knew in the music business. Through them she was introduced to songwriters and musicians including L.A. Reid, Babyface, Oliver Leiber, and Glen Ballard, who would become driving forces in the creation of her debut album.

Her main concern now was to get a deal with a record company. Paula had formed a singing group called the Cheer Girls, an all-girl band with herself singing lead. The idea of being part of a group appealed to Paula, and it was her original concept when she set out to record a demo.

"I had saved some of the money I made as a choreographer, and my idea was to go into the studio and put my own demo tape together," she says.

With three other female singers, Paula recorded two songs on a demo and sent out her tape to a few record companies. Some rejections came back. The powers-that-be at Motown Records weren't impressed and passed on Paula, declaring there were already too many girl groups on the pop scene. Others weren't looking to sign anyone new just yet, and Paula felt as if her recording dreams might all evaporate before she was given a real chance.

The way she was finally "discovered" occurred while Paula was in New York, working with Duran Duran on their "Notorious" video. Executives who were about to launch Virgin Records' American label invited

Paula to dinner at Indochine. They had never heard her sing, but were nevertheless interested in her. They told Paula they knew her choreography work and asked if she would consider cutting some demonstration tapes. After they heard Paula's demo, the deal was secured—and Paula was on her way.

Like Motown, they didn't like the girl group idea. But they did like Paula's voice and told her they wanted to record her as a solo artist. They had enough faith in Paula to believe she could be a major recording star. They were ready to sign her up, but they warned her that she had to work "very fast." They had to have the album in stores in June, in time for summer sales. Many record executives believe summer songs to be the best-selling songs of the entire year. They would release Paula's first single simultaneously with the album. They just needed the guarantee that she would be able to handle the hectic schedule. She agreed.

As soon as Paula signed her name on the dotted line, the pace of her life suddenly began to quicken. She had only a few months to deliver ten completed recordings to Virgin. She worked at a frenetic speed, recording the tracks for the album *and* continuing with her choreographic work on movies, TV, and with rock stars.

The first time Paula walked into a studio was to record "Knocked Out." "I had recorded it, then I had to take some time off because I had choreography commitments to *The Tracey Ullman Show*, to the George Michael *Faith* tour, and to the movie *Coming to America*," she says. "It was weird for me because I would do all my choreography projects during the day. I would have an hour for a dinner break, and then I would record in the evening until about three o'clock in the morning. It was a very hectic time of my life and the biggest rush. But that's what I was up against when this all happened for me."

Her day's schedule began at 6:00 A.M., when she drove to the Fox-TV studios in Los Angeles to sketch out the choreography for *The Tracey Ullman Show*. Paula designed the steps on this show from the seasons 1987 to 1989, and won an Emmy Award for "Best Choreography on a TV Series" in 1989. On a normal day, Paula spent a full six hours working on the show before leaving the studio at one in the afternoon.

From Fox studios, Paula then dashed over to George Michael's house to help him get his moves down for his upcoming *Faith* tour; then it was over to the set of *Coming to America* on the Paramount Pictures lot at five-thirty. When her job on Eddie Murphy's movie was done for the day, Paula entered a recording studio and laid down the tracks for her own album.

When she had recorded five tracks, Virgin Records began early promotion to make people aware of who she was before her album was finished and ready to hit the stores. Press releases alerted the media of Paula's first solo effort, and Virgin was ready to do a major promotional campaign. It was clear they meant business—now all Paula had to do was deliver the goods.

From the start, she did all she could to stay on schedule and was happy to have the support of such a dedicated group of professionals. With most albums, the artist usually records the songs in one studio, employs one or two songwriters at the most (when they aren't writing their own music), and the tracks are usually produced by one (maybe two) producers. The album's executive producer was Gemma Corfield, but for the tracks Paula worked with six producers who doubled as songwriters and musicians. She also recorded each song in a different studio, which is rarely done in the music business.

She was fortunate to combine her talents with those of L.A. Reid and Babyface for the very first song she would record. L.A. and Babyface wrote and produced "Knocked Out," and took on the roles of musicians as well. Babyface provided the background vocals and played keyboards on the track, and L.A. played drums and percussion programming.

Paula was in impressive company. She recorded "Knocked Out" at Studio Masters and Silverlake in Hollywood, where recording artist Pebbles, Yvette Marine, and Darryl Simons (who co-wrote the tune with

Babyface and L.A.) provided additional background vocals.

Oliver Leiber, whom Paula calls "my hero," wrote and produced three of the hottest songs on the album, "The Way That You Love Me," "Opposites Attract," and "Forever Your Girl." All three were arranged by Leiber for the Noise Club and recorded at Creation Audio in Minneapolis, Minnesota. The Wild Pair, who does a duet with Paula on "Opposites Attract," can be heard singing background vocals on the other two tracks.

Another songwriter, Elliot Wolff, produced and arranged his compositions "Straight Up" and "Cold-Hearted" for Paula. These tracks brought in an entirely new group of people for her to work with. The songs were recorded and mixed by Keith "K.C." Cohen Studios, and the musicians on "Straight Up" and "Cold-Hearted" were Elliot Wolff (drum programming and synthesizers), Dann Huff (guitar), and Delissa Davis (background vocals).

Continuing in her quest for the best new tunes, Paula next worked with Glen Ballard, who produced "State of Attraction," a song he co-wrote with Siedah Garrett. Paula recorded this song at Studio 55 in Hollywood. The musicians and singers on this track were Glen Ballard and Chuck Wild (drums and programming), Basil Fung (guitar), and Angel Rogers and Yvette Marine (background vocals).

"I Need You," which was written and produced by Jesse Johnson and Ta Mara, was recorded in two separate studios; Paula laid down the vocal track at Cochrane Recording in Los Angeles, while the music was recorded at Fantasy Studios in San Francisco. Songwriter Johnson played drums and all keys, Bobby Gonzales and Dave Cochrane played guitars, and Eddie M played saxophone on "I Need You."

Curtis Williams wrote, produced, and arranged "Next to You" and "One or the Other." Paula recorded her vocal track on "Next to You" at the Studio Masters in L.A., and the music was recorded at House of Music Studios in West Orange, New Jersey. Curtis Williams played a very big part on this song. He arranged vocals, mixed the tune with Tim Jaquette, provided synthesizer programming with Randy Weber, and sang background vocals.

He also worked on "One or the Other," arranging the vocal and singing background. This track was mixed by Keith "K.C." Cohen. The musicians who played on "One or the Other" were Bob Somma (guitar) and Jeff Lorber (keyboards).

Paula contributed to the writing of this song and enjoyed the experience so much that she plans on writing more songs. "If I had had more time to work on the first album, I would have written more of the material," she says. "I plan on spending more time on my second album. I want to write fifty percent of it."

Paula was given almost total artistic con-

PAULA ABDUL

trol on her first album, and she wondered about the responsibility that went with the job. If it was a hit, she would be congratulated, but if it failed, the blame would fall on her shoulders. Her only consolation was the input she received from such experienced and talented people. The producer of Paula's songs really helped her put everything together. As one top songwriter expressed, "Paula has a mediocre vocal range. She was greatly helped in the studio by her producers."

She wouldn't think about what might happen now. She herself was happy with the final recordings of each track, but had no idea how her creation would be received by the public or Virgin Records. Upon hearing it, the record company was enthusiastic. But the album wasn't completed yet.

The next—and last—phase of putting it together was perhaps as important as recording the tracks. At least that's how Virgin felt. Paula was scheduled to pose for the photos that would appear on the album cover, and the title had to finally be decided on. It was always a unanimous decision that one of the song titles would be duplicated for the cover. After narrowing it down, everyone thought "Forever Your Girl" said it all.

Not only did Paula show the people at Virgin Records she was talented, but they also recognized a potential star when they saw one. Paula was pretty and could be promoted as a hot pop star. She had the right look and the right attitude. It was going to be easy to publicize her, especially when the right image for her was decided upon.

Though some people at the top wanted her to become the new Madonna or the new Janet Jackson, Paula proclaimed she wasn't going to turn into a carbon copy of another successful singer. She was hoping to become a success all on her own.

When the day of the photo shoot arrived, Paula voiced her opinion on how she wanted her photo to look on her debut as a recording artist. She stated she was most concerned with maintaining a natural look. She didn't want to be heavily made up in any of the photos. The makeup artist, Francesca Tolot, applied a very light amount of makeup to Paula's face before photographer Alberto Tolot took a session of flattering photos. Once the photographs were ready, individual close-ups were chosen for the front and back covers of the final album.

Since Tolot's photographs were excellent, it was a tough decision, but Paula and Virgin agreed on what would eventually become the album's distinctive cover. It is a beautifully lit photograph of Paula, showing light streaming down the left side of her face and shoulder.

Though choosing the right photo seemed crucial to Paula and her record company, it is an old argument in the rock world. Some artists feel it really doesn't matter what kind

"I'm candid," says Paula. "My personality comes out in a way that people understand."
(Photo by Tammie Arroyo/ Celebrity Photo)

Paula with Elton John.
The two top pop stars
appeared together in a
Diet Coke commercial.
*(Photo by Janet Gough/
Celebrity Photo)*

Paula with her proud
parents, Lorraine and
Harry. *(Photo by Scott
Downie/Celebrity Photo)*

Paula won two American Music Awards for Favorite Dance Artist and Favorite Pop/Rock Female. *(Photo by Greg DeGuire/Celebrity Photo)*

Paula and fellow dancer Patrick Swayze were presenters at the 32nd Annual Grammy Awards. *(Photo by Janet Gough/Celebrity Photo)*

At the 62nd Annual Academy Awards, Paula teamed up with Dudley Moore. *(Photo by Janet Gough/Celebrity Photo)*

Singing and dancing at the Palladium in New York City, Paula was resplendent in a favorite black leather motorcycle jacket. *(Photo credit Robin Platzer/Images)*

Paula likes clothes she can move in, and nothing moves like fringe. *(Photo credit Robin Platzer/Images*

Eddie Murphy caught up with our gal at a Hollywood party given by Virgin Records. Paula was awarded a Sextuple Platinum record award. *(Photo by Scott Downie/Celebrity Photo)*

Although she's been romantically linked with sexy *Full House* star John Stamos, Paula says emphatically, "It's just been a couple of dates!" *(Photo by Scott Downie/Celebrity Photo)*

Opposite Left: Paula with her Sextuple Platinum record award for her #1 album, *Forever Your Girl*. *(Photo by Scott Downie/Celebrity Photo)*

 Paula designs many of her own clothes and is always delighted to let photographers take pictures of her newest creations. She favors pants, sparkly tops, and long, dangling earrings. *(Photo credit Robin Platzer/Images)*

of artwork appears on the package because the real test is what's inside.

Because this was Paula's first album, Virgin was hoping the alluring shot of her would attract record buyers. They would soon find out if their theory worked. Paula Abdul's debut album, *Forever Your Girl*, went on sale in June 1988.

Paula's favorite tune off this dance powerhouse is "(It's Just) The Way That You Love Me." It begins the album and makes a very strong and important statement. The song describes a girl's disinterest with her boyfriend's rich life-style, liking him only for the way that he loves her. Simply, she is not a material girl; she is unimpressed by limousines, yachts, diamond rings, fame—all the things that pop-tart Madonna *wanted*— and made other girls want—in her 1985 hit song "Material Girl."

Paula, who feels times have changed over the past five years, says that's what she was trying to convey in "The Way That You Love Me." "Having been behind the scenes of the entertainment business so long, I've seen how much emphasis is put on material things," she says. "But I've learned those things aren't ultimately important, and there are lots of girls out there who aren't chasing after them."

The energetic pace of the first track continues throughout Paula's album. She manages to do an even amount of every style of music on *Forever Your Girl*—pop, rock, R&B,

dance, and rap, all lumped together in one neat and appealing package.

"Knocked Out" is a pop-oriented dance song. "Opposites Attract" is a duet between Paula and the Wild Pair. A mixture of rap and pop, it tells the story of the differences between a couple who seem to be a perfect match despite the fact that they don't share anything in common.

All Paula's songs are about love. In both "State of Attraction" and "I Need You" she is hoping to tell her true love how she really feels. They are both excellent lyrically and musically, and both contain a potent blend of danceable rock. On the instrumental bridge of "I Need You," Eddie M's saxophone playing is outstanding.

"Forever Your Girl" returns to a more pop/rock sound. It's a bright, peppy number in which Paula sings of a relationship rumored to be over. Paula's style is terrific as she tells her guy that she's "forever your girl."

What can be said about "Straight Up" that hasn't already been said? It was Paula's first number one hit and remains one of the best off the album. Once you listen to "Straight Up," you find yourself humming it. It's that kind of song.

With a tempo a bit slower than any other track on the album, "Next to You" is a simple love song, very soothing, and a welcome pop ballad in the middle of a collection of dance tunes.

Back to Paula's distinctive sound, "Cold-

Hearted" is a delicious song in which she tries to warn a girl about the ways of her boyfriend and how she could find somebody better than him. The instrumental bridge on this song almost sounds like a piece of classical music that shouldn't be there, but it works so well into this pure dance cut.

The album ends with "One or the Other," which is Paula's first venture as a songwriter. Showing yet another side of her endless talent, we can look forward to more songs written by Paula in the future.

After *Forever Your Girl* was released, the first thing that started pouring in were the reviews. Paula didn't know what to expect. As it turned out, the overall critical response was mixed but mostly favorable.

Some critics tended to harp on the fact that Paula was a dancer/choreographer and not a singer. One critic wrote, "As a singer, she's a fine dancer." Other critics were impressed by Paula's debut of simmering dance songs. *Billboard* said, "Angelic-voiced Abdul delves high and hard."

After the reviews were printed, all that mattered to Paula now was what the public thought of the album. So she waited, as did Virgin Records. But nothing happened. The first single, "Knocked Out," went nowhere and the album didn't explode the way Paula had hoped. What went wrong? Virgin Records didn't have a clue. They had faith in Paula and the album, so they decided to release a second single almost immediately.

"(It's Just) The Way That You Love Me" didn't do much better than "Knocked Out." Though both songs received some radio airplay, neither reached the Top 40 charts. Back in the late summer of 1988, without having a hit, it seemed as if *Forever Your Girl* was a flop. Paula was in shock; after all the work she had put into it, her album was dying.

She was completely discouraged. It was a very uncertain period in Paula's life. She was puzzled by the failure of the album and the first two singles. She wondered if she should just forget the whole idea of wanting to be a singer and return to choreography, the thing she was so successful at. But Paula wasn't a quitter. Instead of giving up, she began searching for explanations as to why the album wasn't striking a chord with the public. But she could find no answers.

She decided to ask Virgin for the truth on her album. "All I ask from the people I work with is honesty, no matter how much it hurts," she admits. "So I asked, 'Is the record a stiff or what?' And the record company said, 'Paula, it ain't happening.' "

Was Paula's album really a bomb or would there still be some life in it? A third single, "Straight Up," was released exactly six months after *Forever Your Girl* had first hit stores. Things became optimistic when the song made the Top 40 and started to climb the charts.

Straight Up the Charts

"My biggest claim to fame is that Paula once
choreographed me."

—Tom Hanks

The song that propelled Paula Abdul
to superstardom was her third single,
"Straight Up." Just a few weeks before it hit
the charts, Paula had all but given up hope.
She thought *Forever Your Girl* was going to
disappear and never be heard from again.

Of course, the success of "Straight Up"
would change all that.

The single would fan a gust of life into
Paula's career as a singer and thrust her into
the limelight. It was the moment she had
been waiting for, but it came at the worst
possible time in her life.

The week "Straight Up" went to number
one on *Billboard*'s Hot 100 chart, Paula was
in bed with 103° fever and a very bad case
of the flu. The nonstop work had taken its
toll on her. "It was at a time when I was very
run-down and tired," she says, "and I re-

member the record company calling me to tell me I had the number one record in the country. I could barely speak, but I was saying, 'Oh my God, I'm so happy.' "

As soon as the public became aware of Paula's exciting sound, they went out and bought her album to see what the rest of it was like. In a matter of a few weeks, *Forever Your Girl* made the charts as well, eventually bulleting to the number one spot.

Paula's best-selling album is full of fresh, danceable songs, eminently hummable tunes filled with accessible lyrics. Paula, who had searched for a fresh sound, was dedicated to creating an originality on record. And she succeeded.

It was like a dream come true. As her third single vaulted to the top of the charts, it was apparent that Paula's winning voice and attitude were the two things making her a star. She was welcomed with open arms by fans, the media, and other top entertainment figures.

Paula was suddenly the hottest new music star in the country. The approval she had been seeking only months earlier was suddenly hers. Paula Abdul was a *name*.

While her music had people dancing, she was emerging as a major celebrity, but a different kind of celebrity, especially in the field of music. Her sound was clear and sunny; her personality was sweet and shy.

Paula created an image by just being herself. She didn't put on an act for the public or the press. She enjoyed what she was doing and she let everyone know about it. Her maturity, confidence, and sense of fun made everyone notice her.

People wondered where this overnight sensation had come from. It was only later that they would find out how hard Paula had worked to achieve her position at the top of the entertainment ladder. She had been devoted to perfecting her album, working all hours of the night, but she was awed by the response the album received.

"It's unbelievably exciting!" she says. "I feel like I closed my eyes one day, opened them up again, and I was this pop star."

"Straight Up" elevated Paula to stardom beyond her wildest dreams. The song, which wasn't originally going to be released as the third single, was now the track everyone wanted to hear. Paula was thrilled; no matter what happened now, most of her worries were cleared up.

Watching her album rise to multi-platinum status, Paula was amazed when *Forever Your Girl* started selling millions of copies. To date, it has passed the six million mark, and after over one hundred weeks on the charts, it is still racing out of the stores.

"It's the most bizarre thing," says Paula, her voice filled with a crackle of excitement. "I sold 191,000 copies in one day. That's mind-boggling. When they call you with a number like that, you have to start screaming, 'Don't you understand this? This is unbelievable?' "

Paula Abdul had achieved everything she

ever dreamed about—and more. To keep her on the minds of millions, Virgin Records quickly released her fourth single, "Forever Your Girl." The song would also rise to the top of the charts and become Paula's anthem in the process. She became "Forever Paula" to her fans, which she was beginning to gain more of everyday.

Forever Your Girl broke music industry records by producing the most Top 10 singles off one album. It also broke a record previously set by Whitney Houston. For a while Whitney was the only female singer to have three consecutive number one singles from a debut album. But Paula had four number one hits in a row off *Forever Your Girl*.

Having her own fans was a part of the business Paula had been looking forward to. For years she had worked with stars who commanded the attention of many loving admirers. Often Paula had witnessed one of the celebrities she knew stop and sign an autograph for a group of excited fans.

Now with the success of *Forever Your Girl*, Paula was in the public eye. Now she would be stopped and asked to sign her name for someone who admired her. The thought made her think of herself when she was younger and how happy she had been meeting the people she looked up to.

On two separate occasions Paula came face-to-face with her favorite entertainers and remembers how kind and courteous they were to her. "When I was sixteen, I was in a restaurant with my family, and I saw three great stars, Liza Minnelli, Ben Vareen, and Gene Kelly," she says. "They are all singers, dancers, and actors, and I grew up watching them perform in movies. They were sitting at a nearby table having dinner, and when I spotted them, I was floored!

"I waited until they were finished with their dinner, and then I walked over to the table and asked for their autographs. I was very nervous, but they were very nice to me and I appreciated that."

Paula looked at Gene Kelly, who she says has been her main inspiration, and told him of her desire to also become a dancer. She explained to him how she had seen all his movies and decided at a very young age she would pursue a career in dance.

"What's really interesting," says Paula, "is that I met Gene Kelly again this past year and was able to tell him that what I had said to him ten years earlier had come true."

This past November, Gene Kelly called Paula to invite her over to his house for dinner. "He came in, and it was one of the most special moments of my life," she says. "He gave me a big hug and said, 'I feel like I really know you.'"

Since that time, Paula has become very friendly with Gene Kelly and has gone over to his house quite a few times. Kelly's son, Timothy, is a budding director and has discussed a future film project with Paula. But mainly Paula and Gene like talking about dance. "I'm not star struck," she offers, "but he's special."

Another time that stands out in Paula's mind was when she met rock star Bruce Springsteen. "I saw him in a supermarket and went right up to him," she recalls. "I was also about sixteen and I told him, 'I love your music.' He said, 'Thank you very much.' That brief encounter with Bruce let me know that no matter how big a celebrity I became, nothing is more important than pleasing my fans, because they're responsible for my success!"

And that's just what Paula has done. She doesn't run from autograph seekers, nor does she hide when she sees someone point a camera at her. If someone's main enjoyment is to have their picture taken with Paula, she'll oblige, provided she has the time.

"Whenever I'm approached by a crowd of fans, I try to make time for everyone who has waited," she relates. "I'd stand and sign autographs all day if I could, but unfortunately, that just isn't possible.

"But even if I can't sign an autograph for everyone, I at least try to make contact by waving, saying hello, or shaking their hands. I really want my fans to know I care."

Paula feels it is important to acknowledge the people who helped her reach her goal as a performer. After all, it is the public who are buying her records and she doesn't forget that. She has seen some celebrities disregard people who want to meet them, and she feels that is totally uncalled for.

"I've seen popular stars who dodge people who want their autograph. I think that's a very bad approach," she says. "I could never be rude to anyone who listens to my music. I want to try to give them as much as I can!"

Paula had thought of becoming a performer for so long, it was a nice feeling to really be one. She had come a long way from the child studying Gene Kelly's dancing in *Singin' in the Rain*. She had climbed so far from her days as a Laker cheerleader and her mom telling her, "Paula, girls trying to do what you want to do are a dime a dozen." Paula's serious career began the day Jackie Jackson asked her to choreograph the Jacksons' video.

Her achievements had finally led to her own fame. She was proud of the things she had accomplished, but Paula has never taken anything for granted. Even though she was now a star, she began working even harder than she had before.

The success of her album continued when another single, "Cold-Hearted," also burned up the charts to the number one spot. With the public ear now attuned to the sound of Paula's music, Virgin reissued "(It's Just) The Way That You Love Me." This time America was much more receptive to the song praising love instead of material things. The song that had previously done poorly quickly moved into the Top 10.

The succession of Paula Abdul hits was masterfully planned; while one was riding high, still fresh in the public consciousness, another song was released by the crafty folks at Virgin. Paula Abdul music was everywhere one turned. The general public hardly complained; they enthusiastically gobbled anything the record company put out. On the success of "(It's Just) The Way That You Love Me," Virgin released "Opposites Attract," and it, too, started easing up the charts until it reached the number one spot.

In less than one year, Paula was being hailed as pop music's hottest singer/dancer. The honor was largely due to the fact that she made dancing look like fun while she belted out her string of hit songs. Paula Abdul clones were springing up everywhere, copying her style. They wanted to know her secret; they wanted to be just like her.

But they weren't the only fans Paula had. She is one of the few artists who is admired by people of all ages. Her fans include young kids knocked out by her sizzling music; teenagers who love her energy and danceable songs; and a wide range of adults who think of Paula not just as a rock favorite of the minute, but as a serious performer with a long and successful future ahead of her.

Paula had conquered part of what it takes to be a major success in the music business. Her debut album was a certified hit. The other half, the music videos of her singles, would be introduced sporadically with the release of each song.

Forever Your Girl clearly revolutionized Paula Abdul's career. Not only did she have five singles on *Billboard*'s Hot 100 chart, but she also produced seven of the most innovative and superbly crafted music videos of the year.

Video Superstar

"There is a lot of strong Eighties patina on all of Paula's work, with a lot of the two-step and one-step stuff that Michael Jackson started. But at the same time she has a solid respect for the classic musicals like Arthur Freed made for MGM with Fred Astaire."
—Oliver Stone, Writer/Director

Contrary to popular belief, "Knocked Out" did not mark Paula's first appearance on video. Although it was her first starring role and the first video off her *Forever Your Girl* album, Paula actually made her on-camera debut in Janet Jackson's 1986 video "Nasty."

In a cameo appearance, a younger-looking Paula is one of Janet's friends as they walk into a darkened movie theater. Though they are all there to see a movie, Janet is summoned to begin dancing and climbs onto the stage. In a flash, she does a somersault *into* the movie screen. Now part of the film, Janet performs her song. Before the video ends, Paula gets in on the act and dances in

79

the aisles of the movie theater. It's interesting to watch this video today because it is clearly a preview of things to come for Paula.

Back then the medium was brand-new to Paula and the public. Music videos were just three years old, and recording artists were still experimenting with different concepts. Paula had gotten in on the ground floor as a choreographer and watched the music video grow into an idea of astronomically successful proportions.

In a recent interview she said, "I'm really happy I was able to grow behind the scenes. It's strange now that I get to do it myself, but the videos are really the most exciting part of it."

Music videos were introduced to the world in the early 1980s. Quickly becoming a new phenomenon, they would truly shape the future of music. But many people believe the music video wasn't anything more than a variation of something that's always been part of the rock scene.

Some believe they have been around since the beginnings of rock 'n' roll, naming the Beatles and Elvis Presley as pioneers of the video. Some also believe that MTV and its dance show, *Club MTV,* is just an updated version of *American Bandstand.*

But music videos are different. For one thing, they serve as extra promotion of an artist's album without the artist having to go on an extended publicity tour. When England's Duran Duran came over to America's shores to introduce their sound, it was their stylish videos of songs like "Rio" and "Hungry Like the Wolf" which would catapult them to the top.

In 1983, the videos of Michael Jackson's *Thriller* album were all the rage. Paula's slick choreography for Janet Jackson would make her and her *Control* album one of the biggest successes of 1986.

The public's demand to be able to watch their favorite star perform any hour of the day planted the seed of success for MTV.

Paula Abdul's videos would become a permanent fixture on MTV, mostly due to the fact that the cable channel had tracked her career from choreographer to recording artist. She had won the 1986 MTV award for choreographing Janet Jackson's "Nasty."

Paula's main thought when beginning her own videos was to put her dancing talents to use. Like the image she created for Janet, Paula wanted dance to be the center of the action taking place.

"I've got a strong sense of what goes on behind the scenes and what it really takes to get a song produced or a video created," she remarks.

Her first video, "Knocked Out," was directed by Danny Kleinman and is a scintillating dance routine with Paula doing her provocative steps. It was the first time she would choreograph a dance routine for herself, and she said at the time, "It's the ultimate joy to choreograph your own music."

She wrestled with many ideas before deciding on what is shown in the finished product of "Knocked Out." One thing she was most concerned with was "to present a little bit more femininity in the choreography I created for myself."

"When I'm doing my choreography, it happens at the strangest times," explains Paula on some of her methods. "Sometimes it happens while I'm sleeping, and I can do the dance sequence and wake up in the morning and write down things I remember. I dance them out in front of the mirror before my shower, while still in my pj's. It's really strange because I can visualize the whole thing," she continues, adding that for some things she wishes she could wake up in the middle of the night to jot down her ideas.

A more common way Paula creates her dance steps is to go to clubs and see what the latest dances are. "I spend time in clubs, then I go home, where I have a room with mirrors and a hardwood floor," says Paula. "I set up my video camera and I just free-style dance. Then I go back and pick out things and expand from there."

Although Paula works in her dance studio at home on many projects, she has also been known to choreograph steps in small rooms. "A lot of my choreography comes in various small places," she says. "When I choreographed a couple of my videos, I did it in my bathroom, where I can only see the waist up so I never knew what I was doing from the waist down. But I got some of my best work done that way."

Paula feels it's important to make changes with her choreography. When she is given a project, she seriously thinks about what kind of emotion she'd like to display. Then she decides where she wants to work out her routines. Every project is different; sometimes the confinement of a small room works better than an open space. It all depends upon the kind of dance she is creating.

Because dance is so important to Paula, she chose not to go the route of creating a story line for "Knocked Out." The song is a dance tune and Paula wanted the video to consist purely of dance. Though the single of "Knocked Out" didn't knock out the public and climb the record charts, the video was the beginning of something Paula says she did not expect.

She would choreograph and star in six more videos over the next six months. The second promotional video was for her second single, "(It's Just) The Way That You Love Me." It was filmed to boost sales of the album and the single.

"The Way That You Love Me" marked the first video award-winner David Fincher directed. He would become Paula's favorite director and work with her on every future project.

Paula and David, who have the highest regard for each other, are a dynamite working team. "The two of us together have a really good chemistry," says Paula. "I trust him very much. David understands conceptually what I want to get across."

Fincher contributes many ideas to Paula's videos. For "The Way That You Love Me," he came up with "the idea of using a lot of product shots and incorporating that as the opposition of what I'm trying to sing about," says Paula, "showing that it's not the material things, it's the way that you love me."

There would be two different versions of this video. The first one, released when the song was first released as a single in 1988, employed six dancers. The second was shot in 1989 when the tune became a Top 10 hit. The themes of both videos are similar, showing a succession of material things like Visa Gold cards, black limousines, computers, champagne, jewelry, etc. But Paula dances in the first version, whereas the second is simply a series of close-ups of her singing. In fact, Paula introduced tap dancing in the first version of "The Way That You Love Me." She would repeat tap in subsequent videos, ultimately adopting the title "tap dancer extraordinaire."

Paula's videos have been praised for their polished look. In every one she evokes an emotional response from her audience. Even though she doesn't direct them, she is involved in the making of every video from the idea to the final cut. She comes up with some of the concept ideas and all of the visual images, beginning, of course, with every dance step filmed. Then she brings in experienced director David Fincher to add his special touches and turn her visions into celluloid reality.

Once all her dance steps have been carefully sketched out and everyone is on their marks, filming begins. This part of the creative process is what Paula enjoys most.

"I get very excited about being in front of a camera," she confides, "because I can be a little more daring or coy. I can be whatever I want to be. When a camera turns on, you either feel really comfortable or you don't. When it turns on for me, I turn on."

After finishing production on her first two videos, Paula didn't begin work on her next one immediately. It was only after receiving word that "Straight Up" had reached the Top 20 *Billboard* charts that Virgin Records and Paula were pushed to film a video of the song. "It showed that the song could be a smash on its own," Paula proudly says.

The video of "Straight Up" would create yet another image of Paula Abdul. First of all, it was shot in black-and-white. "Originally, I was skeptical about using black-and-white," says Paula, "but now I'm so used to it that when color is brought in and I see myself in color, I say, 'I don't know.' "

It's true that black-and-white added a new dimension to "Straight Up." The video is basically a collection of clips showing close-ups of Paula and shots of her dancing. She does every kind of dance movement, from a fast tap introduction to shuffling easily along through twists and turns and leaps.

In some parts, words of the song flash across the screen. There's also passing shots of a juggler, an acrobatic dancer à la Fred Astaire (wearing a hat and using a cane as part of the dance), a musician twirling a bass and, if you look closely, you'll spot Arsenio Hall making a cameo appearance.

Paula asked Arsenio if he'd come down and appear in the video and he did. The filming of "Straight Up" occurred exactly at the time Arsenio was starting his own show and he just improvised. "He got out there and started acting crazy," says Paula. "He was lip-synching to my song and we just captured some real fun parts."

After "Straight Up" Paula was on a video roll. She immediately began thinking of what she wanted to do visually with the title track, "Forever Your Girl." "It's a completely different song," she says, "and I wanted a video that showed a lighter side of Paula."

If anything shows what Paula is really like, it's the "Forever Your Girl" video. Here we see Paula teaching a bunch of kids to dance; we see her wearing glasses behind the scenes; and we see her performing. Filmed in both black-and-white and color, Paula describes the "Forever Your Girl" video as "magical."

Working with kids was the main reason why this project remains Paula's favorite. "I could be with kids twenty-four hours a day," she says. "They have a way of lifting your spirits, and just their innocence and their candidness is so amazing. Half the time I didn't want to leave. If I had to get my makeup or my hair done, I'd have the people come on the set because I enjoyed watching the kids so much. They are so inventive and so creative."

The video is not really a finished product, but that's the charm of it. We see Paula rehearsing the kids, trying to teach them each step, and we see her setting up each scene. The snippets of scenes spliced in reflect a parody of music videos, including everything Paula has done so far. In the role of the motorcycle dude from her "Straight Up" video is a seven-year-old boy named Trevor, who ultimately had a crush on Paula but didn't know how to show it at first.

He followed her around the set until finally getting up the nerve to ask for her phone number during a lunch break. When Paula laughed and told him she was a lot older than he, he just said, "It's okay, I like older women."

Paula remembers the auditions of "Forever Your Girl" to be as much fun as the actual shooting. The kids just had her and David Fincher laughing from the moment the auditions began to the day the filming ended. Paula was present at all the tryouts. With each audition she was able to get new ideas for what she wanted to put in her video.

Her favorite story is the day two boys came in to do a tap routine which she says they had to have had rehearsed about eight

million times because they knew it by heart.
"They had me rolling, laughing hysteri-
cally," recalls Paula, "and they had David
laughing too. The objective of the whole
routine was who could tap faster than the
other one. So they'd start going very fast. It
was so funny because the tap routine got so
frantic. I said, 'We have to incorporate this
into the video.' "

When it came time for Paula to start
thinking about a video for another hit single, "Cold-Hearted," she was yearning to
bring out yet another change in style.
"Cold-Hearted" is perhaps Paula's greatest
effort as a dancer. Her nice-girl innocence
in "Forever Your Girl" transforms into a
storm of sex and spice in "Cold-Hearted."

It was created out of her love for the late
Bob Fosse's movie *All That Jazz* and the
scene in that movie called "Erotica." Fosse
once made a comment about Paula's choreography which was quoted in *People* magazine. He singled her out as the best of the
new choreographers and explained how
much he admired her style. It was her ability to be unpredictable that impressed
Fosse. In her "Cold-Hearted" video, she
pays tribute to him and his style.

"Cold-Hearted" is the only one of Paula's
videos with a slight story line. It begins as
four producers are walking into a building
prepared to see the rehearsal of a routine
they will be shooting that evening. When
one of the producers asks, "Have you seen
this dance?" another answers, "I haven't,

but it's a Bob Fosse thing. It's going to be really, really hot." "Yeah, but tastefully hot," says another.

As they proceed to the room where the dancers (including Paula) are waiting to begin their number, one producer comments, "If there's any problem, we can always make changes."

They walk in and sit down. Paula turns, then claps her hands to get the dancers on their marks. The video begins. The dance is superb. While it may have been drawn from Bob Fosse's "Erotica" dance, the style is pure Paula at her absolute best. The dance is cogent and sexy and, at some point. shocks the four producers as they watch Paula's and the dancers' saucy, seductive moves.

"Cold-Hearted" was shot in an old barroom, which had its advantages and disadvantages. One disadvantage was the fact that the floor was not equipped for the kind of dancing Paula had choreographed. The floor was sticky and had to be mopped down with soap and water before the dancers could glide across it.

Paula had an accident while shooting "Cold-Hearted." In the video she does a knee slide, and because of the problems with the floor, she went sliding airborne on her back right on her tailbone. "It hurt so bad," says Paula, "but all I could do was laugh because it was so embarrassing."

When "Cold-Hearted" was completed, Paula was happy with the results. It was a project she believed in, feeling the visual change would enhance her already successful career. The steamy video certainly adds a new level of interpretation to the lyrics of the song.

Paula had everyone in awe of her exceptional talents, but her seventh video, "Opposites Attract," set the world on its ear. Her inspiration came from the Gene Kelly movie *Anchors Aweigh,* in which he dances with MGM's cartoon mouse, Jerry (of Tom and Jerry fame). The idea of mixing live action and animation has always amazed viewers, including Paula. It is a technique that began in the 1930s, but "The Worry Song" from *Anchors Aweigh* was the first time animation and live action were combined in a choreographed piece.

It was Gene Kelly who thought of the idea in 1945 and convinced the studio head at MGM it would work in the movie *Anchors Aweigh.* And, naturally, it worked perfectly.

Paula had always loved Kelly's dance with the animated mouse, so she set out to do an updated version of the idea. In "Opposites Attract," Paula plays opposite a cool, rappin' cat named MC Skat Cat. There is an utterly delightful, joyful dance between Paula and MC. She wanted to choreograph the number so the cartoon cat would be synchronized with the live action. When the two were matched together, it would give the impression that Paula and the cat were dancing together.

Beginning with a carefully prepared storyboard, the long, laborious process began. To date, this was the only video Paula worked on without the help of human dancers. This time all her co-stars were animated.

After Paula's dance was filmed, the dance of the cat was animated to match her moves frame by frame. In the end, the two figures were optically linked for the final fun presentation.

Paula received rave reviews for the creative use of animation in her video. Her animated co-star, MC Skat Cat, quickly became a favorite with audiences. Says a smiling Paula, "He's pretty popular. They want to give him a record contract where he will be making more money than me."

As a choreographer, Paula is a true innovator. From the beginning of her career she wanted to do more than just be popular, even more than just dance. Paula wanted to create numbers in which the dancer does with his body what an actor does with words. She strove to devise a language of dance that would replace the song's lyrics and tell the audience what *she* feels and thinks. Paula's visions are always to "write" her own characters with her movements.

With her videos Paula has the urgency to succeed, to surpass herself, and to get better than the best out of the dancers she hires. It's always been important to Paula to be able to hire people on their talent alone. When she was starting out, all dancers were

5'7" and taller. Because she was 5'2", it took her awhile to get noticed, and now she hopes to prove that a dancer doesn't have to be tall to be successful.

"When it came time for me to audition dancers, I started hiring a lot of shorter dancers," she says. "I was hoping it would be part of my influence to show everyone that the performance is what counts. The strain and stress of being taller isn't as important anymore."

Paula's ambitions are tremendous. She constantly desires to reach beyond herself; she wants to stretch her talents as far as they can go. She has been given the chance to prove what she is capable of doing through her videos.

Story lines never mattered to Paula. More important to her is a good performance. In her videos she is exceptional, exercising her accomplished steps into motion. Paula is one of the most energetic dancers around. She works so hard on her routines that viewers are apt to sweat just watching her.

Paula Abdul proves how stimulating her dancing really is. Her choreography is carefully staged and includes an enormous amount of zeal. Her flashing footwork and rhythmic perfection in all seven videos is unmatched by anyone else. It is apparent how much Paula enjoys working on her videos.

Not only does she have a one-in-a-million talent, but she also has a million-dollar screen presence. Paula is more than an ordinary one-dimensional star. There are hidden qualities, inner secrets that make audiences want to see more. Paula's dance style is a mixture of everything from ballet to jazz. She fuses traditional tap dance with more classical styles.

She has been working in this medium for so many years, choreographing so many videos, that Paula can be called one of the pioneers of dance in videos. She has created a veritable dance revolution.

If you really take a good look at the evolution of the dance crazes of the late 1980s, they came about as a result of Paula's choreography for people like Janet Jackson (with the invention of the Snake dance) and ZZ Top (with the Egyptian-styled Velcro Fly dance).

Paula doesn't let herself get trapped into one style when she is working on a new project. She is most concerned with expanding into new areas and showing that she is capable of a lot of different styles. With each video she embarked on, Paula tried to bring out something new. By lining up her videos of "Knocked Out," "The Way That You Love Me," "Straight Up" and "Forever Your Girl," you see an enduring body of work. On video her presence is a strong and important one.

In December 1989, Virgin Music Video released a mass-market video tape called *Paula Abdul—Straight Up*. It includes documentary footage plus Paula's videos, "Knocked Out," "Straight Up," "Forever

Your Girl," "Cold-Hearted" and the two versions of "(It's Just) The Way That You Love Me." "Opposites Attract" was still in production and, unfortunately, couldn't be included on the tape. But that didn't stop sales. Within the first few weeks of its release, *Paula Abdul—Straight Up* went to number five on the Top 10 Video List.

Paula had achieved success in all circles of the music business. Through the widespread appeal of her album and videos, Paula Abdul's place in the world of pop music has been securely confirmed.

Pop Princess

"At Laker games, it was clear she had talent. Paula is
a fighter. She gets what she wants, but somehow she's
managed to stay one of the world's sweetest people."
— Jackie Jackson

Nineteen eighty-nine will go down in the
history books as the year of Paula Abdul.
Not only had she scored big with her debut
album, but now she was receiving awards
for her triumphant success.

The first of many extraordinary nights for
Paula was the sixth annual MTV Video Music Awards held on September 6, 1989. The
evening was a remarkable personal and
professional victory for Paula as she as-
cended to the podium four times, winning
for her video "Straight Up."

In the past six years, the MTV Awards,
which honors excellence in videos, has become a glamorous, star-studded event similar to the Grammys, Oscars, and Emmys.

On that night, Paula drew the biggest
screams from the audience. All her fans

agreed: Success couldn't have happened to a more deserving person.

Accepting her awards, she responded with a lot of emotion as she looked out into the audience cheering for her. Although the honor of winning an MTV award wasn't new to Paula (she won Best Choreography for Janet Jackson's "Nasty" video in 1986), it somehow felt different this time around.

She was somewhat composed when she won the first award. Walking up the stairs to the microphone, Paula clutched the statuette and said, "Thank you, all of you, thank you so much. Wow, this is exciting." But as the night progressed and her name was called three more times, Paula's enthusiasm exploded and she delivered an emotional response, thanking the people who had helped her realize her dream.

"You don't want to see me weep because that's what's going to happen," she told the audience. "This has been a really great night."

MTV's Julie Brown, the hostess of *Club MTV*, a show Paula appeared on, said before announcing Paula as the winner of yet another award for "Straight Up": "Not only has she danced her way to the top, but she's done it with number one singles—it's Paula Abdul."

Paula was ecstatic and couldn't hide it. Her fans yelled vociferously and she responded by saying affectionately, "I love all of you."

Before leaving the stage, she added,

pointing to the audience, "This one goes to all of you who love to dance."

In total, Paula went home with four MTV awards for "Straight Up." Individually, the awards were for Best Female Video, Best Dance Video, Best Choreography in a Video, and Best Editing of a Video.

But Paula didn't merely sit in the audience and accept trophies. She also performed on the MTV Awards. Paula rocked the house with a three-song medley, "(It's Just) The Way That You Love Me," "Straight Up" and "Cold-Hearted." Her saucy, tantalizing dances provoked MTV to periodically run this segment of songs as a video on the 24-hour-a-day cable channel.

Backstage in the press room, Paula was a little dazed by the entire night, as she told reporters, "I can't comprehend it! I'm still trying to capture the moment!" Later she said, "I won't really have time to feel it. I've become a bit of a workaholic. I'm going to start my second album."

As television audiences watched Paula win the bulk of the night's awards, they were also awaiting the commercial breaks.

Reebok had signed Paula as their spokesperson for the company's new line of Double Time Dance shoes. And the commercials debuted during the MTV Awards.

Paula sings her big hit, "Straight Up," while she dances wearing the Reebok shoes. The company promised buyers that they'd be dancing just like Paula. The dance shoes offered solid support and the kind of flexibility an athlete or dancer must have. Reebok's dance line is made of garment leather and synthetics and comes in a variety of colors.

Besides filming the television commercials, Paula appeared in print ads in magazines for Reebok. The words surrounding a photo of Paula wearing her Reeboks blasted the lines: "Millions of girls want to be in her shoes. But she wants to be ours."

Paula's happy-go-lucky personality was perfect to reach out to consumers. Though the advertising executives at Reebok were the first to sign Paula to a contract of print and television ads, she was also recruited by Michael Beindorff, vice-president of Coca-Cola's advertising for a Diet Coke commercial.

It is a well-known fact that Pepsi and Coke have a pop war going on concerning today's hottest personalities. It all started back in 1984 when Michael Jackson appeared in the widely publicized Pepsi commercials. Ever since, David Bowie, Michael J. Fox, Fred Savage, Kirk Cameron, Tina Turner, and Robert Palmer have joined the Pepsi Generation.

Over at Coke—or Diet Coke—rival stars Whitney Houston, George Michael, Roger Rabbit and Bob Hoskins, New Kids on the Block, and those award-winning spots with Art Carney and Brian Bonsall (as his inquisitive grandson) were also selling a lot of soda.

The money paid to an entertainer for an

endorsement is staggering, as high as $5 million. But the people at Pepsi and Coke say it's worth every penny in securing the soda business' yearly $100 billion in sales.

Many of the biggest names in the rock world have been approached to add their own flavor to this shrewd form of media promotion. With Coke still holding the number one position as the favorite soda, Paula set out to do her commercial for Diet Coke.

Signing Paula to do the commercial was a feather in the cap of the soft drink manufacturer. With Elton John as her partner in the ad, Coca-Cola expected this commercial to be a powerful weapon in its battle to sell more soda than Pepsi.

While Paula attracted the younger viewing public, Elton appealed to an older group, and together they became a magnet for cola drinkers everywhere to reach for a can of Diet Coke.

It is an especially eye-catching duet with pop star Elton John. As he pounds on the piano singing the Coke jingle, Paula is dancing on giant-sized keys of the piano. Her dance is like an updated version of the spectacular production number in the 1937 musical, *Ready, Willing and Able.* In this film starring Ruby Keeler, a set was designed to look like an oversized typewriter and had Keeler and co-star Lee Dixon tapping on the keys. Typewriter keys were transformed to piano keys for the Diet Coke ad with Paula supplying her own style of choreography.

The Diet Coke commercial aired for the first time during the American Music Awards and made Paula the official new celebrity spokeswoman for Coke. She was now in the league of other hot stars who did Coke commercials, but differed from some of them because she really *likes* the soda. An insider reported, "Some people lend their names to products without being big supporters of the product, but Paula told us it's her favorite."

The commercial generated a positive response and gained a phenomenal amount of interest. Television stations across the country unanimously decided to air the commercial during the telecast of the American Music Awards show.

The night the commercial debuted, the huge budget and nerves to get the spot on the air in time dissolved into its ultimate triumph. Coke's Beindorff had once again made an excellent choice in choosing Paula.

When her excitement of viewing the commercial ceased, the business of winning an American Music Award got underway. Inside, the fans were screaming for Paula, who was nominated in several different categories.

Because the awards are based on the sales of records during the year, the balcony was filled, as it always is, with zealous fans. But this year the fans' screams were louder than usual. On some occasions it was difficult to enjoy the show and hear what some stars had to say in their acceptance speeches.

Paula won two American Music Awards for Favorite Dance Artist (ironically winning over her competitor and friend Janet Jackson) and Favorite Pop/Rock Female.

Backstage in the press room, she said, "This is wonderful because it's the people who appreciate what I'm doing. It's the fans' support. They've given me a lot of joy and I'm glad I'm able to reciprocate."

In February 1990, Paula's success continued. The recording establishment itself, somewhat selective in its willingness to recognize achievement, didn't overlook Paula at the 32nd Annual Grammy Awards on February 21. She received one nomination for Best Pop Female Vocalist. Although she lost the award to Bonnie Raitt, Paula was proud to be included in the category.

In an interview, Paula expressed her feelings on what awards really meant to her. "Awards are always a nice recognition of your hard work," she says. "I don't place too much importance on awards. It's wonderful to be nominated and if that's all I am is nominated, I'm happy. If I happen to receive an award, then that's even better."

RIAA (Recording Industry Association of America), which certifies success in very tangible terms, gives platinum records, CDs, and cassettes to an artist who sells more than one million copies of an album. Two days after the Grammys, on February 23, Virgin Records held a star-studded party in Paula's honor at Pazzia Restaurant in West Hollywood. They were celebrating the six-millionth sale of *Forever Your Girl.* At the party Paula was presented with a sextuple platinum record.

The huge award displayed Paula's album cover in the center surrounded by six platinum CDs and six platinum albums. At the bottom, her five Top 10 singles were placed neatly in a row, a line of 45's and a row of cassette singles of "Forever Your Girl," "Cold-Hearted," "Straight Up," "(It's Just) The Way That You Love Me," and "Opposites Attract."

At the party Paula's eyes filled with tears as she was handed a microphone to thank her record company for the party and the opportunity they had given her. "Everyone at Virgin Records, I thank you from the bottom of my heart because you believed in me when no one had to," she began emotionally. "You really took a risk with me and I appreciate it. You helped me live out my dreams. And my management," she said, glancing back. But when Paula's eyes met the eyes of her managers, she started to laugh, exclaiming, "I feel like an idiot." That moment showed how real Paula has remained. There is nothing phony about her. The fact that she isn't just another plastic, stamped-out star is the reason why she has gained such fame.

Paula has won most of the awards she received nominations for. Her track record in 1989 and 1990 has been unbelievable. No one before had ever been awarded so many different trophies in the span of one year.

PAULA ABDUL

On March 11, 1990, she was named Favorite Female Musical Performer at the People's Choice Awards, beating Janet Jackson, Debbie Gibson, and Madonna.

Paula Abdul told one reporter, "This has been the most phenomenal time in my life. It's been like catching my breath because it's only been in the last two months that it has all really hit. I never expected all this. It's been an incredible year. Every day I pinch myself."

In the press room of the American Music Awards, Paula was asked, "What if it all ended tomorrow?" "Well," she began, "if it all ended tomorrow, no one could take away what's happened this year and the joy that it's brought me."

In the fast-lane music business, a performer must spread out his talents from recording to filming videos to performing live. Paula had accomplished two out of three. The one thing missing in her life was embarking on a tour. It is the part of the music business entertainers enjoy most.

And now Paula was ready to take the next step in her career and perform her music live in concert.

Onstage With Paula

"At the Grammys, people were knocking me down to get to her."

—John Stamos

"**W**hen I hit the stage, there's no feeling like it. Nothing compares to going out there live," says Paula Abdul.

She creates a fantasy onstage. When she is dancing and singing her hit songs, she eliminates barriers for herself by sheer intensity and concentration. In Paula's performances the wall between herself and her audience vanishes. In an almost magical way the two sides of the footlights become one. The viewer watching Paula's dance moves begins to believe she is actually experiencing what she is relating onstage.

She projects that kind of magic. Some artists were made for the stage. In Paula's case, the stage was made for her. From the moment her name is announced, the entire audience erupts into a frenzy of applause.

Late in the summer of 1989, Paula got her

first taste of performing in concert. Because she hadn't gone on a real tour with her album, she decided to star as the headliner of a short concert tour sponsored by MTV.

MTV's Julie Brown brought her show on the road. A kind of rock revue, it showcased the talents of up-and-coming stars Tone-Loc, Milli Vanilli, Was (Not Was), and Information Society. The tour also featured *Club MTV* dancers on go-go platforms. The concert was a cavalcade of commercial dance hits and proved how dance music was literally taking over as the dominant sound of music.

Paula put together a seven-piece band for the show, and hired background singers and dancers. "We had a twenty-three-person entourage with my tour and all twenty-three people got along so great," she says. "We loved each other so much. We all would go to dinner together, we all would go to lunch, we all would go to a movie together on our off days. The camaraderie that we had made it so special. And all of that just went onto the stage."

Paula traveled to several cities with the tour and played in many stadiums, including a show in her own hometown at the Los Angeles Forum. Yes, Paula went back to the place where she had spent four years as a Laker cheerleader.

Adding to her opening night jitters was the old feeling of being back in the Forum, where it all began for her. "I remembered all those nights when I'd arrive at the Forum and the other girls would be coming from school and work and we'd go out on the floor and knock all the weird tunes out," she says. "Then we'd have dinner at the cafeteria. I always remember the smell of the lockers and the coldness of the place. On the night of my concert, I was walking through the tunnel and it was freezing. I kept flashing that I wasn't going out there to perform in my uniform, I was going out to go up on the stage as the *star*. It was the most amazing, amazing thing."

Everyone from the San Fernando Valley turned out to see their homegirl, Paula, whose riveting stage performance blew the roof off the Forum. Backstage before the concert began, Paula was taking sips of water. She nervously waited to hear her name announced and tried to busy herself until the time came. She could hear a low buzz of excited conversation rise to a crackle. The house lights dimmed; applause was mounting, a chant of "We want Paula" was filling the auditorium. And suddenly, before she knew it, the music began playing and she was onstage.

Paula was bowled over when she spotted her family clapping their hands to the beat of her music. By the closing chords of the final encore, tears of emotion had welled up in everyone's eyes—including Paula's.

Her performance was a powerhouse of energy. Yet despite the dazzling physical routines she staged for her songs, her concert was very personal. Paula maintains a one-

on-one relationship with her audience:
When she is up onstage, she has everyone
believing she is performing directly for
them.

Her gestures are purely musical and intensely intimate. Her show is full of pep and
zest. And she gets her audience involved—
dancing and singing along with her.

Paula so obviously enjoys what she's doing that the good time she's having onstage
becomes infectious. She is aware that the
crowd is there to be entertained—and she
does her job well. Paula feeds off audience
response. To her, they are the most important element in her performance, and the
audience's applause and screams only make
her want to do more.

At the time of her concert on the *Club
MTV* tour, Paula said it was the most incredible feeling. It's almost as if a transfusion of
energy flowed between her and her audience. When they react to her music enthusiastically, it only makes the concert more
exciting and fun.

She had been very nervous putting her
tour together because it was the first.
"When we were getting it ready, I just kept
hoping all the puzzle pieces would fit into
place," she says.

During the tour Paula discovered a way of
dealing with the stress of being on the road
by taking up jogging. Every morning she
ran for two miles; while keeping her mus-
cles toned, she also exercised her vocal
cords by singing her entire set during the

run. "It helped to build breath control and stamina," she says.

Paula will never forget her first concert tour; it's been indelibly implanted in her mind. What her fans want to know now is when Paula will be going back on the road.

When will she go on a worldwide tour and give her fans around the globe the concert they've been waiting for? Soon. "As soon as I finish my next album," she says. "I'm going to be doing a big worldwide tour. I'll be going everywhere."

The Paula Abdul Style

"Had Paula mentioned the words 'Double Platinum' back when she was a cheerleader, people would have called her crazy, but the little cheerleader beat the odds."

—Arsenio Hall

The verdict is in: The people who know Paula Abdul agree she's as nice as everyone says. The sudden burst of fame she has achieved hasn't gone to her pretty head. Paula is still as level-headed as she was before all this happened.

In public, Paula is a photographer's dream, an electrifying performer, a woman of many diversified talents. Paula has established herself as a successful dancer, choreographer, singer, and possibly future actress. She is a beautiful young woman, inheriting her exotic looks from her father's side of the family. Paula's dad is Syrian-Brazilian and her mom is French-Canadian. Paula is talented, she wins awards, and she goes to par-

111

ties with gorgeous eligible bachelors. She is living the life of a star!

But what about when the lights dim and the cameras stop rolling? What is the real Paula Abdul like in private? For one thing, she is refreshingly natural, down-to-earth, and shy. She has a rapierlike intelligence and shrewdness. When you talk to Paula, she is extremely honest and willing to express her innermost feelings.

In interviews, she never shies away from any questions. Paula is quick and witty. Her conversation is full of eminently quotable phrases. Sometimes she giggles while she talks, but she's also serious and determined and comes across as someone who is certain of what she wants.

Jackie Jackson says of Paula, "She is a fighter. She gets what she wants, but somehow she's managed to stay one of the world's sweetest people."

Paula aims to do as she pleases as far as her career is concerned, and she does it all with her feet planted firmly on the ground. There are no simple answers to what Paula Abdul is all about, and she seems to like it that way. One minute you feel as if you know everything about her; then she bounces back and shows another side of herself.

The way Paula dresses and fixes her hair has audiences paying attention to her. Paula's image is somewhat wholesome and engaging, but there is a sexiness to her style as well. Her videos, for example, ooze sex appeal. Says Paula on this subject, "I have an exhibitionist streak in me, a freedom to express all the different sides to me. Sexy is definitely a part of me."

Freedom means a lot to Paula, freedom to believe as she wishes, dress the way she wants, and climb as far in her career as she can. She's firm in her idea of who she is and what she wants, unshakable in her perception of her goals and image. She's ferociously independent; she is never swayed by other people or manipulated.

Paula describes herself as being very "energetic, determined, sentimental, and emotional." Her weakness, she says, is getting overly sensitive in a situation. When people praise her work, Paula can't help responding in an emotional way. "Sometimes I'm so embarrassed because I start to cry," she says.

While Paula sings rap-influenced rock, it is interesting to note that the music she likes to listen to is the stuff Manhattan Transfer and Stevie Wonder sing. When Paula went to the Songwriters Hall of Fame Awards in Radio City Music Hall in 1989, she was cornered by the press, who asked her what her favorite song was. "You Are the Sunshine of My Life," she said, "I love that song!"

Paula's success came upon her—and us— at rocketlike speed, and many wonder why she's become such a powerful performer. Part of the reason may be due to the fact that Paula possesses a positive-thinking philosophy. She claims her success is not much of a surprise, even though she is dazzled by the fact that her debut album outsold her competition. Yet one way or another, Paula always knew something like this would happen because she always believed in herself and her talents. She is a passionate believer in working hard at your dreams and becoming anything you want to be.

The ability to believe in herself, Paula says, is what has kept her going through the times when her future didn't seem so bright. The goals she set for herself years ago have all come true, and she is just beginning to reap the rewards of years of dedication.

Despite her dizzying success, Paula Abdul never pulls the star treatment routine on anyone, from her family to her friends to her band to the dancers she hires. Paula is not a hard person to work for. She'll give everyone a certain amount of freedom to perform their job well. "I have the ability to be patient with the entertainers I work with so they feel confident and comfortable about achieving what they have to do," she says.

Paula becomes friends with all the people she works with. She doesn't consider herself above them because she is now the star. To Paula, it's a group effort that makes her dances come to life. Without the support of the other dancers, these carefully planned pieces of choreography would be nothing.

Paula treasures the early support she received from people like the Jacksons and Janet Jackson. They worked with her; they didn't make her feel like she couldn't handle the position she was chosen for. It gave her the confidence she needed to really do a good job, and that's how she feels about the people she works with today.

They may feel intimidated about being choreographed by Paula because of all the publicity she's received. She has an excellent reputation in the business, known for being a perfectionist and working all hours until she gets it right. This could make a new performer a trifle nervous and Paula understands that.

"I'm very friendly," she says. "I learned from Janet Jackson to really get to know the people you're working with. Janet and I became very close friends."

To hear some people talk, there's a major feud going on between Paula and Janet. The word is that they are rivals now and bitter rivals at that. But they say none of it is true. Even though Janet lost an American Music Award to Paula this past year, she reveals, "I'm very happy about Paula's success. She's like a sister to me, and there's no competition between us."

Why does Paula Abdul have such universal appeal? Her asset is that she communicates with people. Through the things she chooses to project to the public, they detect a sincerity in what she says. No matter what Paula may continue to achieve, she still has a strong bond with her audience.

"I'm candid," she says, smiling. "My personality comes out in a way that people understand; they feel that I'm approachable." Paula is being looked up to as a role model and becoming a trendsetter of the latest fashion.

Throughout history, music and fashion have always seemed to complement each other as both continue to change with the passing of every year. Music is the symbol of the sound everyone wants to hear for the moment. Whether it is rock, soul, pop, or rap, it often emerges as the new trend, the sound more people are buying. And it's the same with fashion. There is always someone influencing styles being worn. For young people the influence comes largely from music stars.

In 1985, Madonna created a new wave of fashion as girls began copying her sloppy, carefree look. Today they all want to dress like Paula. Unlike Madonna, Paula's style is fun and chic; the clothes she chooses to wear are very stylish. She likes wearing a variety of fashions, from beautiful beaded dresses to jeans and a tank top.

As one of the best-dressed female rock stars on the scene today, Paula enjoys the fact that she is making a strong fashion statement. She admits she never thought it would happen because her style has always been so unconventional. Paula has become a trendsetter by just wearing what she feels comfortable in.

As for beauty secrets, Paula really doesn't have any. In fact, when she is asked this question, she laughs, "Twenty-hour days with no sleep. That's my secret."

In the morning Paula washes her face with

cold water only. She prefers the natural look, but does apply a light amount of makeup to her face, especially when she does a photo shoot. She uses natural, peach, and rose blushes and eyeshadows, midnight blue or brownish-black eyeliner to bring out the brown of her eyes, and all shades of red and peach lipsticks. Paula's favorite nail-polish colors are clear, white, and red, and she keeps a supply of all three in her home.

As for jewelry, Paula admits, "I have a weakness when I pass a jewelry counter." She spends most of her money on earrings, all different shapes and sizes. "I'll wear every kind of earring, but big hoops are my favorite," she says.

Her hairstyles are constantly changing. She'll wear her hair in ponytails or piled up on top of her head, using fun accessories like clips, elastic bands, or bows. These days Paula prefers wearing her hair longer, combed down and draped over her shoulders.

As far as the color Paula thinks looks best on her, she says, "I tend to lean toward brighter colors—blue, red, yellow. But I also wear some darker colors like black and brown."

When Paula was younger, she'd wear different colors to catch attention. She remembers her early days of struggling to become a dancer, but being told 5'2" tall was too short. "It was almost impossible!" she recalls. "The dance producers would line us all up, and all they'd see is the girls who were 5'6" tall and up. And there I was 'little Paula,' just trying my best to stand out. I had to work really hard to get noticed. One of my plans in the early days involved wearing different colors.

"Everyone in the dance chorus would come to the auditions wearing nice black leotards, so I decided to show up in red and black. I needed something to stand out from the tall girls."

The greatest thing about Paula's success and her attitude is that she's been able to hold it all together. But how does she do it? What is Paula's secret remedy for handling success and not letting it change her? "I have been able to keep steady through all this by staying close to my family and trying to keep close to the people who loved me before I became a star," she offers.

Paula had her own apartment for a while, but decided to move in with her married sister, Wendy, when success came her way. "I was working so much and when you come home by yourself and just come home to sleep . . . well, I missed my family life. I was losing sight of my nephews growing up."

There's no denying the fact that family and close friends remain high on Paula's list. Now with her new three-bedroom house being renovated, she spends half the week with her mom and the other half with her sister.

Paula and Wendy are very close and always have been. When Paula was a guest on Arsenio Hall's show, she told him, "I worshiped my sister when we were growing up. I followed her around everywhere and did everything she told me to do." That included a funny little incident when Paula was nine years old and Wendy was sixteen.

Paula confided in her older sister that she was concerned her breasts would develop as large as Wendy's had. Her ever loving sister decided to play a joke on Paula and explained that they wouldn't if she rubbed Vaseline on them every night and blew on each one three times.

Innocently, Paula took her sister's advice and performed this ritual for two weeks before her mother caught her and grounded Wendy.

The two talented siblings are now going into business together as Paula and Wendy ready a dance studio scheduled to open in Los Angeles later this year. Paula is moving her office into the building, where she will rehearse most of her new dance routines. Paula is also looking to hire professional dance teachers to give lessons in her new studio.

Dance is becoming such an important part of everyone's lives today. Both adults and teenagers are finding themselves caught up in wanting to learn the new steps.

Besides having a desire to dress like Paula, budding dancers are emulating her cool dance steps as well. Dean Barlow, who was Paula's first dance teacher when she was a little girl, is the first to comment on this new surge of interest in what is being commonly referred to as the Paula Abdul style. Barlow has been a dance teacher in Hollywood for

seventeen years and says he's never had so
many requests for one style of dance before.

"You see a new Paula video come out, and
a week later the kids on *Soul Train* and *Club
MTV* are doing her same steps," says Barlow. "I can't tell you how many times I get
calls from little girls saying they want to
dance like Paula."

The fact that Paula has been able to take
her dancing and mix it with a saleable collection of songs is what excites her. She is
happy with her title of pop culture heroine.
"Who would have thought that a pop star
would integrate tap dancing into the mix?"
she exclaims. "Now *that* is the coolest thing.
There is now a shortage of tap teachers at
dance studios across America." She is hoping to fill that important void by hiring some
tap teachers for her new dance studio.

Paula proudly refers to dance as "no longer a spectator sport. Kids place a lot of importance on dance these days. Instead of
games and sports, they are getting into
dance-offs." Paula is also aware of the fact
that all this has happened over the past few
years since she hit it big with her choreography. "I don't want to sound in any way,
shape, or form cocky," she says, "but I feel
a part of all that. I guess I'm a good example
for young people to see that with a little
hard work, you can really achieve whatever you want in life. It makes me feel good
that people look at me and want to do what
I'm doing. It's great to be an inspiration to
someone else!"

Romance Rumors

"Even though she'd outdanced everyone, Paula never fit anyone's idea of a tall, leggy dancer."
— Lorraine, Paula's mother

There is no way Paula Abdul can avoid being linked with different men in the gossip columns. After all, she's a star and she's single. That puts Paula in open season.

Every time she's seen out on the town with an eligible bachelor, the news usually reaches the papers that she's involved in a hot new romance. Whether these rumors are true or false, they are splashed in newspapers and magazines for all the world to see.

This kind of publicity basically comes with the territory of being in the public eye. Rumors of romances between stars have been going on since the days of silent movies. Sometimes there is truth in the stories circulating; other times the people involved are just friends who had their picture taken at a party.

The most important thing about these stories is that the fans are getting what they want: to read about their favorite star's private life. Since Paula can't escape or stop the rumors, she has learned to live with them and laugh them off.

First, there were the stories linking her to a secret relationship with Jackie Jackson. Then came the Arsenio Hall romance rumors.

They began when Paula's single "Straight Up" brought her fame. The talk of a romance started when Paula invited her friend Arsenio to the set of her "Straight Up" video. He made a cameo appearance in the video and from then on, they always seemed to be together.

Whenever Paula won her early awards, Arsenio was there to congratulate her. They loved teasing photographers, dodging the flashbulbs and hiding their faces from the cameras. Their public displays of affection were all the gossips needed to make Paula and Arsenio Hollywood's newest romantic couple. The rumors started to fly the minute their picture was snapped and were fueled by Arsenio's own rise to stardom as the late-night talk show host of *The Arsenio Hall Show.*

Though both have denied the rumors, Arsenio decided to give the media mavens a run for their money. He decided to have a little fun with his "romance" with Paula.

In a way, he kept it going longer than it normally should have. "He said we were married and I was the mother of his three children on television," says Paula. "He loves playing jokes on me!"

For the next few months Paula was barraged with questions about her hot and heavy romance with Arsenio. She kept denying it, but the rumors continued to spread.

When she sat down to talk to the press, the question was always brought up. "It's all completely made up," she told one magazine. "Arsenio and I are close friends, and I have an extreme fondness for him, but there's nothing, absolutely nothing going on."

In another magazine she explained, "Arsenio loves to tell the press that we're married and things like that. We really care about each other a lot, but his career is his thing. It's his marriage and in a sense, it's mine too. I'm very much committed to my career, but it doesn't mean that eventually I wouldn't be willing . . ."

Even Paula's mom commented on the reported romance between Arsenio and her daughter. "Arsenio is a nice guy," Lorraine said. "But for God's sake, can't a girl have a close friend without people making more than really is there?"

The truth is, Paula and Arsenio are very close, longtime friends who admire each other a great deal. When they met, Paula was a Laker Girl and Arsenio was a struggling young comedian. It's been a very rocky road for the two of them. After years of trying to be recognized, both Paula and Arsenio reached the top almost at the exact same time.

Arsenio, who is extremely ambitious, admits that Paula beats him ever so slightly in this department. Hall is an actor, comedian, writer, singer, and terrific talk show host, and while all that is enough for one person to handle, Paula is juggling more in her career.

"She is representative of a new breed of entertainers, something I call the 'invasion of the talent monsters,' " says Arsenio. "It's like the old days of the studios, where to be a star you had to be able to do a little of everything, like Fred Astaire or Judy Garland." Hall, who calls Paula a kind of Everywoman, continues, "There are white teenagers who look at Paula and relate to her as they do to Madonna. Then there are black teenagers and they can relate to the way she moves. Unlike Madonna. Okay, Madonna can shake it up, but she ain't no Paula Abdul. *She* shakes it up the way we shake it in the ghetto. And that is saying something."

There is clearly a strong bond of respect and love between Paula and Arsenio, but no real romance, at least not right now. As the stories linking the two were ending, they were only the beginning of a series of romance rumors for Paula. Subsequent rumors came in spurts. After a photo of Paula sitting on the lap of rap star Tone Loc at an MTV private party at L.A.'s Spice restaurant appeared in a magazine, it caused eyebrows to raise. But that was basically the end of that.

On the grapevine of Hollywood gossip, whenever one rumor ceases, another is usually waiting to be revealed. Paula is astonished by the stories that circulate about her. She doesn't understand where they originate from. "The other day my makeup artist told me that he'd heard I'd gotten collagen injections in my lips," says Paula. "He also told me that he'd heard I'd gotten a boob job. It was funny to me, but also upsetting. Then he said, 'Honey, all this means is that you've arrived.'"

Maybe that's some explanation to the rumors involving her new "romances" with Michael Jackson and Prince. Paula has the highest respect for both performers and says she'd like to work with them in the future, but there's no romance with either Michael or Prince.

"I heard the one where I was supposed to be living in the Gloved One's mansion," she says. "Michael supposedly said that everything he owned was mine. But then I heard that Prince had stolen me away. I've never been alone in a room with Prince in my life. Just meetings."

In the future Paula may be dancing up on screen with Michael and Prince, but assures everyone her relationship with both of them will be strictly professional.

Paula still feels like she has plenty of time to settle down. She looks forward to the day she will get married and start raising a family, but honestly confesses, "At this point in my life it would be impossible." Most of Paula's time is reserved to her busy work schedule. Friends have dubbed Paula the hardest-working person in show business because of the hours she devotes to her career.

"I don't have time for a boyfriend, honestly," she offers. But that doesn't stop her family and friends from introducing her to future prospects. "I'd love to see Paula marry and have children," her mom told *People* magazine, then asked, "Do you know anybody nice?"

In order to make her family happy, Paula says, "I had lunch with someone my sister fixed me up with. Between my managers and friends, all I hear is 'God, Paula, there are so many guys who would love to take you out. They're just intimidated or they think you must already have a boyfriend.'

"Or they tell me that it's the girl's responsibility to take the initiative," continues Paula, who has her own stories to tell. Though her success has given her lots of influence in the dance world, it's meant she's had to dance alone in her private life.

Paula has found that men don't ask her out because they *are* intimidated by her fame. At dance clubs she has discovered men are actually *afraid* to dance with her.

"When I go dancing with my friends, I only dance with them because it seems like no other man would come up and ask me to dance," Paula explains. "I think they assume that I'm going to start dancing the way I do in my videos or the videos I've choreographed for other artists."

Recently, Paula has been seen around Hollywood with John Stamos, the handsome actor from ABC's *Full House.* Are they dating? Many wanted to know the answer to that question, especially since Paula arrived with John at the Virgin Records party held in her honor and at the Grammy Awards.

So what's the story? Well, at this time Paula is only saying, "I don't want to make too much out of it. We've just been on a couple of dates, that's it."

John, on the other hand, has gone as far as telling the press he and Paula share many things in common. "At the Grammys, people were knocking me down to get to her," he says, then goes into detail describing the traits they share.

"We both go to bed early and we both have horrible allergies," says Stamos. "I think we discovered we're both a couple of geeks."

Will John and Paula's relationship intensify? Only time will tell. They *are* dating. But for now John remains one of Hollywood's Sexiest Bachelors, according to *Us* magazine, and Paula remains Hollywood's Most Wanted Woman according to *People* magazine. Whether or not Mr. Right is in Paula's near future remains to be seen.

She does admit her personal goals are as

important as her professional goals, even though she's spending more time on her career right now. "I want to have the security of settling down," she confesses, "but it's not my time to do that right now. I've learned that whenever I've tried to get involved with someone in the whole dating process, you have to put a lot of time into it. I don't have that quality time. But it doesn't mean I don't want to be in love and get married and have kids."

Paula says one day when the time is right, she'll put time into a relationship. Until that day comes, Paula is happy with her success and resigns herself to her all-work, no-fun schedule.

Although she has been on a few dates with Stamos when they find the time, Paula is concentrating on her career. "I'm really excited about what's happening," she says. "Right now I'm very career-oriented."

The Price of Fame

"Paula is a real sweet girl."

—Eddie Murphy

There are two sides of success just like there are two sides of a coin. For all the good things that Paula was enjoying in her career, she wouldn't be exempt from experiencing the dark side of fame. Though she tends to look on the bright side of every situation, Paula was dealt a harrowing blow this past year.

Although there has been some good timing involved in building her into the success she is, Paula has always been willing to take whatever risks were necessary to do it her way. The willingness to go a little further, along a different route, is a major part of Paula's success story. What she's done by taking chances has put her at the top of her profession.

But success spawns publicity. And as Paula's star continued to rise, she was now in the center of a new kind of publicity, the kind most stars have to deal with at one time or another. The subject of her income was brought up. The gossips never tire of conjecturing about how much celebrities are raking in.

Money had never really meant that much to Paula. And when it starting pouring in, she didn't go on wild spending sprees. The two things she has splurged on have been her new three-bedroom home in the Hollywood Hills and her convertible black Jaguar.

Out of Paula's earnings come salaries for her management, dancers she hires, her publicist, and other assorted personnel. She's never been really impressed by money, and by no means is it the key to her happiness. It's merely security.

While Paula doesn't wallow in her super success, she does worry over the loss of privacy her popularity has brought. It is symptomatic with people in the spotlight who are easily recognizable. For a writer or producer, personal privacy is much easier to maintain. They are not routinely recognized when they walk down the street. But for an actor, athlete, or musician whose picture is constantly plastered all over magazines and posters, it's completely different.

In the beginning the lack of privacy never really bothered Paula. She didn't feel violated by it—until the night of January 22, 1990, the night of the American Music Awards.

Held at the Shrine Auditorium in Los Angeles, the awards telecast had been eagerly awaited by the performers nominated and the fans who bought their records.

All of music's luminaries were dressed-to-the-nth for the gala event. Paula looked especially stunning that evening; she was wearing a beautiful black-and-white dress with a pearl-and-beaded trim.

With all of rock's royalty in attendance, it was Paula who got the show off to a rousing start by opening it with a splashy performance of "(It's Just) The Way That You Love Me." For the well-staged number Paula hired seventeen dancers, whom she later treated to dinner. Since she couldn't get them into the party after the AMA awards, Paula decided to take them to Chaya Brasserie.

The night was nearly perfect. Paula had won two awards and went home feeling very elated. But what she found when she opened the door of her Studio City condo shattered all the excitement. While Paula was at the American Music Award show, her condo had been burglarized. The thieves seemed to know exactly where Paula kept all her valuables. By the time she returned home, they had taken her stereo, thousands of dollars in jewelry, some clothing, makeup, platinum albums, and several of her awards.

"I was heading straight for the phone machine, but when I flipped on the light, it was gone," says Paula. The police were immediately called, and after she gave them the details of what she found missing, detectives began an investigation.

The whole incident upset Paula, but what topped it off was a tip to the media. The TV news found out about the robbery at Paula's home almost immediately and began splashing the news all over the tube. Before Paula could even tell her mother exactly what had happened, Lorraine had already heard about it.

"I was even more upset by that," Paula says. "It struck me as terribly weird that it was important for everyone to know. For the first time I felt really scared."

Paula's life had now gone completely public, and after that night's experience she wondered if the honor was a blessing or a curse. Things had drastically changed for her. She always accepted the fact that she had gone from a modest behind-the-scenes choreographer to a mega-star, but now she questioned her popularity. Had her life become too public?

Too many people knew her now and some found out where she lived. It was hard to escape. But it all went with the job, and Paula was well aware of that fact from the moment she first stepped onto a stage.

Becoming a well-known celebrity certainly has its good and bad sides. Yet according to Paula, there are definitely more pluses than minuses in her life.

Even though it isn't easy for her to always understand the amount of attention being bestowed on her, she can't ignore it. Her superstar status seems a bit unreal, and sometimes Paula finds herself standing back and looking at it as if it were happening to someone else.

She still giggles like a kid when she walks into a supermarket and someone stops her. "Once I was at the market and these girls spotted me and just started screaming," she says. "My hair was slicked back and I was wearing jeans, but they still recognized me. They got embarrassed about screaming, but told me, 'We really love you.'"

The love she is receiving from fans today is staggering. She receives over five thousand letters a week, including marriage proposals. In addition to working on her music career and choreography, Paula's life has become a succession of photo sessions, press interviews, and personal appearances.

Her success has inspired diverse reactions from close friends and family. Some worry that it has all happened too fast and she is pushing herself too hard. But at this point in Paula's life, things couldn't be better. She has been given more self-confidence by having more people believe in her.

Paula, at age twenty-seven, is even becoming a popular teen star and appearing regularly on the covers of the glossy fan magazines. With her popularity on the rise, the requests for interviews began pouring in from all publications.

Paula didn't ignore the teen magazines. She gave as much time to them as she did to

People, Us, and *Rolling Stone,* among others. In a way, she liked expressing her feelings about her teenage fans and giving them advice in their own lives and ambitions. It was an important gesture on Paula's part to be cooperative with the teen magazines because she has a teenage niece and nephew.

Paula's sixteen-year-old nephew proudly told his aunt he is now the most popular kid in his class. And her thirteen-year-old niece is rapidly becoming the most popular kid in her class because she gives Paula's phone number out to friends.

"I get these calls," Paula says, grinning, "and when I answer, I hear these screams: 'Oh, God, it's her!' "

As for her little three-year-old nephew Alex, well, he's Paula's biggest fan *and* toughest critic. Alex isn't at all interested in listening to nursery rhymes; he likes only his aunt's music.

"It's so funny because Alex knows every word to every song on my album," exclaims Paula. "When his friends come over, my sister says that he puts in my video and says to his friends, 'Auntie Paula.' It's the cutest thing!

"Alex has his favorite songs off my album," she continues. "The last time I saw him, he told me exactly what songs he likes and what he didn't like."

Paula has often been asked her advice on breaking into show business and she readily provides an answer. "My advice to anyone who wants to break into this business is to keep working hard, keep true to what's inside of your heart, and be patient," says Paula, adding, "Good things come to those who wait."

Good things have definitely come to Paula Abdul. Even though a few unpleasant incidents were thrown in as part of the package deal, the rewards of her success have been great.

Breaking into Movies

"You see a new Paula video come out, and a week later the kids on *Soul Train* and *Club MTV* are doing her same steps.

—Dean Barlow, Paula's First Dance Teacher

Paula Abdul *is* going to be a movie star. And if you don't believe that, just ask the major producers in Hollywood and the executives at Warner Brothers, who are clamoring for Paula to sign to her first film.

In meetings with her, they have already matched her up with co-stars like Kevin Costner and Clint Eastwood. They are ready to put Paula up on the big screen without ever knowing the answer to the question: Can she act?

Her friend, Arsenio Hall, has already stated, "I know Paula can act. I've already seen her act madder than she actually was at the time just to get the effect."

Though it's a tempting proposition and Paula definitely wants to launch a movie career, she isn't interested in it until she finds a role she believes in. Because her career as a choreographer, dancer, and recording artist has been such an unprecedented success, she is especially cautious in her choices. She says her career as an actress will start slowly.

"I want to start small," she says. "I'm not looking to jump into the movies and make mine a short career. I really want it to last."

Offers for Paula's own story to be brought to the silver screen arrive at the offices of her agents every day. But Paula will have nothing to do with that idea.

She is ready to make her move into movies; it's just a question of finding the right project. Amid her hectic schedule, she's been reading—and rejecting—scripts on a regular basis in her search for the right vehicle.

Paula is quite adamant about not doing anything if it doesn't seem right to her. She has a definite idea of how she would like to be portrayed on the big screen. She has always been a fan of the movies, especially musicals. They represent so many things to her. Since her interest in movies and theater is equaled by her passion for dance, she'd like to bring back the days of the musical movie for today's generation. Paula sees dance only getting bigger in the years ahead, especially athletic dancing.

Paula Abdul seems to go one step further than the most diversely talented stars. Like any self-respecting would-be superstar, she became a pop/video music idol.

She now plans on spreading her creative wings in a theatrical direction. In addition to her plans to try her hand at acting, Paula also plans on continuing to choreograph future projects.

A few years ago, she said in an interview that she admired the talent of Debbie Allen. "My ambition is to be an all-around performer like her," Paula explained. "She's my inspiration; I would love to follow in her footsteps."

Since then Paula has achieved her goal, showing so much talent of her own that Debbie Allen paid *her* a compliment. After watching Paula perform at an NAACP function, Debbie told her, "I can learn something from you!"

At a time when Paula's slightest whim becomes a reality, it is obvious she can and will accomplish every goal she sets for herself. Less than ten years ago, Paula was dreaming about a career as a performer. Today she is one of the most popular performers on the scene. She is a celebrity, a superstar.

There isn't a day that goes by without someone mentioning Paula's name. She is so famous today that she creates a sensation everywhere she goes. Dance clubs play her music and everyone tries to duplicate her dazzling footwork. Photographers follow her into premieres and parties and snap rolls of film.

Paula Abdul is on top—and that's exactly where she intends to stay. She is not interested in being part of anything that will exploit her in any way. Her goals right now are limited to working with people who care about producing quality work. One of those people is writer/director Oliver Stone.

He is the man behind blockbuster movies like *Platoon*, *Wall Street*, and *Born on the Fourth of July*. Stone is interested in making powerful films, the kind that will mean something years down the road. He's already proven that and has been awarded with Oscars for his efforts.

Early in 1989, Stone personally selected Paula to choreograph the movie version of the Broadway musical *Evita*, based on the life of Eva Peron. After a few years of other directors and producers trying to bring *Evita* to the screen, it almost looked as if it was going to really be done this time.

But this project seems to have a dark cloud hanging over it. Everyone at one time or another has been linked to *Evita*.

First, Steven Spielberg was interested in directing. Then a host of actresses publicly announced they wanted to play the juicy but demanding lead role. Everyone from Barbra Streisand to Madonna was mentioned as being in the running.

When Oliver Stone announced his planned adaptation, he started fresh and held auditions. Meryl Streep desperately wanted to play the part. She even went as far as recording her singing voice to prove to Stone that she could provide her own vocals. She convinced him and was set to star.

Stone then hired Paula, who impressed him with her talent. People questioned how he knew someone as young as Paula would be able to handle the choreography of this big-budgeted movie musical, but he never had any doubts. "I just had a hunch about Paula," he says. "There is a lot of strong Eighties patina on all of Paula's work, with a lot of the two-step and one-step stuff that Michael Jackson started. But at the same time she has a solid respect for the classic musicals like Arthur Freed made for MGM with Fred Astaire."

Paula excitedly put everything in her career on hold for *Evita*. But suddenly all plans for the movie were cancelled, and Paula was very disappointed when she was given the news.

"That was a six-month commitment from me," she says. "It's no longer happening. My passion was to do this. It meant so much to me, you don't even know."

Oliver Stone immediately plunged into his next scheduled movie, a film biography of Jim Morrison and the Doors. Wanting to still work with Paula, he called her and asked her if she'd be interested in choreographing this film instead.

For Paula, it kind of eased the pain of losing her shot at working on *Evita*. "I'm a big fan of Oliver Stone's," she says. "We didn't get to work on *Evita* together, and he wanted me to work on his movie about Jim Morrison and the Doors. Val Kilmer is playing Jim Morrison and he's incredible. He's so believable in the role."

Paula is completely happy with her position as choreographer of this eagerly awaited movie. As far as her acting career goes, she will continue to search for the right part. She doesn't mind waiting because she knows that somewhere along the way she'll be offered a part she simply can't turn down.

"If I could say what I want to happen to me over the next ten years, I would love to say that I successfully made a film," she confides.

With her agents and numerous Hollywood producers working on Paula's screen debut, it's apparent her acting career will be launched in the not-too-distant future.

Today and Tomorrow

"She went through lots of rejection, but she had the drive and determination."

—Lorraine, Paula's mother

"I'm doing exactly what I want to be doing right now," says Paula Abdul. Today, Paula stands at the pinnacle of her profession. She has achieved so many of her goals, it leaves one to ask what she will do next.

Paula has a long list of future projects on her agenda. Even though she loves where she is right now, there is always something else Paula has her eye on accomplishing. She is clearly focused on her next step and what it will bring to her already flourishing career.

With talk of a future in movies and a worldwide tour in the planning stages, Paula is booked solid for the next several years. Her primary concern right now is her new album, which she is diligently working on.

Until it hits stores, Virgin Records has released an album of remixed versions of her hit singles. The album, entitled *Shut Up and Dance*, is to keep her fans happy as they wait for her follow-up to *Forever Your Girl.*

So far Paula has only announced that she is writing fifty percent of the songs on the new album. Whereas *Forever Your Girl* was a collection of light dance tunes, she plans on tackling some serious issues on her next album like the homeless. One song that will be included is an anti-apartheid song named "Cape Town."

"I'm looking forward to extending," she says. "But I won't deviate too far from what has worked."

Paula seems to have a pretty good grip on the foibles of fame. Since she admits to being a workaholic, the fact that she has to move double or triple time to accomplish all her future jobs doesn't faze her in the least.

"I love to work," she admits. "If I'm not working on a project, I'm in a meeting leading up to the next project. I'm most creative working under the gun."

She continues to search for new avenues to expand her horizons. Paula does not confine herself to one area of show business; rather, she plans to be successful in all areas. Paula is determined to continue experimenting with every aspect of show business—writing songs, acting, singing, dancing, choreographing new routines. She is not interested in resting on today's accomplishments, but trying even harder for tomorrow's.

Paula realizes she made it to the top in a fairly short time, and now she must continue to work to remain there. Unlike some celebrities, Paula doesn't intend to take any time off and relax. She is constantly on the move.

She is using her success to map out a careful plan for the future, one filled with advancement. She has stated that it takes a lot of determination and hard knocks sometimes to become successful. But it takes a greater amount of drive to remain successful.

What has made Paula's journey to stardom a little easier was her belief in herself and her work. Paula took chances with her dancing; she risked everything by breaking the rules. And she created a new style of dance.

But in the beginning it didn't look like she would break the mold dancers were in. "When I started with my choreography, I had the desire to mix technical training with street funk. But people were laughing, saying, 'That's not going to work,' " she says. "But it was something I believed in."

Paula decided the chemistry of the two would blend into a perfect mix. She decided it *would* work. And she was right. Eventually the skeptics congratulated her on her efforts.

"I'm not saying not to take the advice of other people, because everyone's opinion is worth something," says Paula. "But you have to weigh it out and carefully measure it and mix it up with ninety percent of what you believe in. When success does happen, no one can take that away from you.''

Paula is driven, sometimes compulsive. She is bent on developing her talents in the years ahead and shaping her future until she is completely satisfied.

This go-getter explains, "There is a lot more I want to do. I'd like to direct and star in a Broadway musical."

But she has plenty of time to explore other areas of performing before she lends her talents to the Great White Way. The future growth of Paula Abdul could be one of the greatest show business stories of the next ten years. She has been so prolific throughout her career so far that her future only looks brighter.

Her vitality and creativity are immense. She is athletic, charismatic, and ingenious, a performer whose talents reach cinematic dimensions. Bette Midler, Cher, Madonna, and Diana Ross have proven that a music idol's appeal can be successfully translated to a movie screen. Paula Abdul may have a greater physical range than any of the others.

She is a seasoned professional with solid skills. Though Paula admits superstardom is a relatively new phenomenon, she proves she can handle her success and any future challenge with ease. For Paula, the opportunities are vast; on a day-to-day basis she carefully decides what would be a wise career move.

One was choreographing the two Oscar-nominated songs from the movie *The Little Mermaid* on the Academy Awards telecast. After audiences viewed Paula's spectacular numbers, she and actor Dudley Moore presented the Best Song Oscar. Her appearance at the Academy Awards was a vital part of Paula's introduction to the movie industry.

Hard-working, hip, level-headed, and intelligent, Paula Abdul can clearly write her own ticket in Tinseltown nowadays. Her future can be anything she wants it to be.

With so many different avenues open to her, the sky's the limit for Paula Abdul. It's obvious she will go as far as her dreams will take her!

Appendices

Discography

Paula Abdul—Forever Your Girl
  (Virgin Records, released June 1988)

Tracks

The Way That You Love Me
  Words and Music by Oliver Leiber
  Produced by Oliver Leiber for the Noise Club

Knocked Out
  Words and Music by L.A. Reid/Babyface/ D. Simmons
  Produced by L.A. & Babyface for Laface Productions, Inc.

Opposites Attract
  Words and Music by Oliver Leiber
  Produced and arranged by Oliver Leiber for the Noise Club

State of Attraction
Words and Music by Glen Ballard and Siedah Garrett
Produced by Glen Ballard for Aerowave, Inc.

I Need You
Words and Music by Jesse Johnson and Ta Mara
Produced by Jesse Johnson for J.W.J. Productions, Inc.
Co-produced by Dave Cochrane

Forever Your Girl
Words and Music by Oliver Leiber
Produced and arranged by Oliver Leiber for the Noise Club

Straight Up
Words and Music by Elliot Wolff
Produced and arranged by Elliot Wolff
Co-produced by Keith "K.C." Cohen

Next to You
Words and Music by C. Williams, K. Stubbs, S. Williams
Produced and arranged by Curtis Williams for Willpower Productions

Cold-Hearted
Words and Music by Elliot Wolff
Produced and arranged by Elliot Wolff
Co-produced by Keith "K.C." Cohen

One or the Other
Words and Music by C. Williams, D. Pain, P. Abdul

Produced and arranged by Curtis Williams for Willpower Productions

Singles

Knocked Out
(It's Just) The Way That You Love Me
Straight Up
Forever Your Girl
Cold-Hearted
Opposites Attract

Paula Abdul—Shut Up and Dance
(Virgin Records, released May 1990)

The tracks on this album are all remixes or new mixes of Paula's previously recorded tracks appearing on *Forever Your Girl*.

Tracks

Cold-Hearted (Quiverin' 12″ mix)
Straight Up (Ulti-mix)
One or the Other (New 1990 mix)
Forever Your Girl (Frankie Foncett mix)
Knocked Out (Pettibone Mix)
The Way That You Love Me (Housefire edit)
Opposites Attract (New mix)
1990 Hits Medley (New mix)

Videography

Music Videos

Knocked Out
Directed by Danny Kleinman

(It's Just) The Way That You Love Me
Directed by David Fincher

Straight Up
Directed by David Fincher

Forever Your Girl
Directed by David Fincher

Cold-Hearted
Directed by David Fincher

Opposites Attract
Directed by David Fincher

Video Cassette

Paula Abdul—Straight Up
(Virgin Music Video, distributed by Atlantic Records, released December 1989)

Contains segments of candid interview footage with Paula Abdul speaking about her life, her music, and the five videos included in this videocassette. Produced and directed by Jonathan Dayton and Valerie Faris.

Knocked Out (Re-edited version)
Directed by Danny Kleinman

(It's Just) The Way That You Love Me

PAULA ABDUL

Directed by David Fincher

Straight Up
Directed by David Fincher

Forever Your Girl
Directed by David Fincher

Cold-Hearted
Directed by David Fincher

Paula's Vital Statistics

Full Real Name: Paula Julie Abdul
Nickname: "P"
Birthdate: June 19, 1963
Birthplace: Los Angeles
Height: 5'2"
Weight: 105 lbs.
Hair Color: Brown
Eye Color: Brown
Parents: Lorraine and Harry Abdul
Sister: Wendy Mandel (married)
Current Residence: West Hollywood
Shoe Size: 7

Choreography Highlights
TV: The Tracey Ullman Show (1987–89)

Film: She's Out of Control (1989)
The Karate Kid Part III (1989)
Bull Durham (1988)
Coming to America (1988)
Running Man (1987)

Videos: Steve Winwood's "Roll With It"

(1988)

ZZ Top's "Velcro Fly" (1986)

Janet Jackson's "Control," "Nasty," "What Have You Done for Me Lately," and "When I Think of You" (1986)

The Jacksons "Torture" (1984)

Favorite Actor: Eric Roberts

Favorite Actress: Cher

Favorite Movies: *Moonstruck, Dominick and Eugene, Broadcast News, Singin' in the Rain, All That Jazz*

Favorite TV Show: *The Tracey Ullman Show*

Favorite Band: Manhattan Transfer. "They've got great showmanship and they're versatile."

Favorite Color: Red

Favorite Food: Chinese

Favorite Drink: Diet Coke

Self-Description: "I'm outgoing when it comes to the business, determined, sensitive, yet shy."

What She Likes Best about Herself: "It would be the ability to be patient with the entertainers I work with so they feel confident and comfortable about achieving what they have to do."

What She Likes Least about Herself: "The times when I become over-sensitive in a situation."

Biggest Influence on Her Life: Gene Kelly. "He's truly my favorite. He's been so kind and supportive of my career."

PAULA ABDUL

Future Plans: Paula wants to write more music, act in a movie, and a Broadway show.

Awards

Emmy Award (1989)
Best Choreography of a TV Series—
The Tracey Ullman Show

MTV Awards (1986)
Best Choreography—Janet Jackson "Nasty"

MTV Awards (1989)
Best Female Video—"Straight Up"
Best Dance Video—"Straight Up"
Best Choreography in a Video—"Straight Up"
Best Editing in a Video—"Straight Up"

American Music Awards (1990)
Favorite Dance Artist
Favorite Pop-Rock Female

People's Choice Awards (1990)
Favorite Female Musical Performer

American Dance Awards (1990)
Choreographer of the Year

Secret Facts

When Paula was a kid, her father would take her to UCLA basketball games, where she'd see Lew Alcindor tearing up the boards. Years later, when Paula was a Laker cheerleader, Lew returned to Los Angeles as Kareem Abdul-Jabbar.

If she could choreograph any star, Paula says it would be Steve Martin.

People would be surprised to know that Paula dances for her own enjoyment. She loves going to dance clubs because she says that's where she gets her creative ideas.

Singer Michael Bolton has known Paula most of her life. He used to babysit her when she was a child.

Paula feels that by working with six different producers on the tracks of her debut album, she was able to reflect something that's distinctly her own.

Even though Paula was born and raised in California, she says her favorite city is New York because "the excitement is unmatched!"

Paula Speaks Out

On Doing It All
"I don't see why you can't do it all. I grew up studying and loving the old MGM musicals, where you had to be an all-around entertainer. Ever since I was a kid, I wanted to do it all. I loved choreography, but I wanted

to be a performer. My idols were people who could do many things—sing, dance, act, choreograph."

On Recording Her Debut Album, Forever Your Girl

"I've really grown tremendously this past year. I've learned to take risks. It was a pretty scary move to record my first album. For a while I thought, 'Okay, I like the album, but will anybody else?' But once I put aside all that emotional stuff and really focused in and believed what my heart was telling me, I was able to really go for it and be a success!"

On Her Favorite Type of Guy

"I like guys who are sensitive, very positive, and confident. I like someone with a sense of humor. I love to laugh. I think it's important!"

On Her Personality

"I'm candid. My personality comes out in a way that people understand. They feel that I'm approachable."

On Janet Jackson

"Janet is my prize student. She worked her butt off for me. The end result is that we made each other look extremely good."

On Her Choreography

"My choreography suits men very well, and the women who can do it are damn hard, strong dancers. It's extremely athletic and it combines a careful balance of femininity but also 'I can do what the guys can do.' When I choreographed that style for Janet, it worked really well for her and it went with the music. I present a little bit more femininity in my choreography for myself."

On Breaking into Movies

"I don't want a film that's going to star Paula Abdul. I want it to be the kind of thing where people will look and go, 'Oh my God, that's . . . Abdul is in that film."

On Filming Videos

"I get very excited about being in front of a camera because I can be a little more daring or coy. I can be whatever I want to be. When a camera turns on, you either feel really comfortable or you don't. When it turns on for me, *I* turn on."

On Being a Laker Girl

"I was this cheerleader who kind of broke the rules. I wanted to kind of get rid of the pom-pom thing, focus more on dance."

On Arsenio Hall

"I can talk to him about anything. He means a lot of different things to me in my life. He's the one person I can tell exactly how I'm feeling, and he can understand it because he's either going through it or he's gone through it."

On Success
"I never take anything for granted. I feel like I closed my eyes one day, opened them up again, and I was this big pop star. It's unbelievably exciting!"

On Working
"I'm more or less a workaholic. I get antsy when I'm away from work too long."

On the Future
"I'm not in this for the quick buck. My goal is long-term, quality work."

Where to Write to Paula

Paula Abdul
c/o Virgin Records
9247 Alden Drive
Beverly Hills, CA 90210

Paula Abdul Fan Club
Mail Mann
14755 Ventura Blvd.
#1-710
Sherman Oaks, CA 91403

About the Author

Grace Catalano is the author of two consecutive *New York Times* best-sellers: *New Kids on the Block* (Bantam) and *New Kids on the Block Scrapbook* (NAL/Signet). Her other books include *Kirk Cameron: Dream Guy*, *River Phoenix: Hero & Heartthrob*, *Alyssa Milano: She's the Boss*, *Teen Star Yearbook*, *Richard Grieco*, and *Fred Savage*. Grace is currently the editor of three entertainment magazines, *Rock Legend*, *Dream Guys*, and *Dream Guys Presents*. She also wrote *Elvis: A 10th Anniversary Tribute* and *Elvis and Priscilla*. Grace lives on the North Shore of Long Island.